GOLF RULES ILLUSTRATED

COMPILED BY
THE UNITED STATES GOLF ASSOCIATION

RULES INCIDENTS BY
GARY A. GALYEAN

ILLUSTRATIONS BY
**PETER DAVIDSON
AND HELIX DESIGN PARTNERSHIP**

hamlyn

Foreword

"The Rules of Golf are indeed a beautifully balanced code, rich with logic, drama and the traditions of a great sport." Richard Tufts, *The Principles Behind the Rules of Golf*.

Unlike most sports that are played on regularly defined areas, like tennis courts, football fields or baseball diamonds, golf is a game played over a vast and irregular area. Indeed, a golf course is a slice of nature itself, marked by remarkable changes of terrain and natural phenomena that lead to unpredictable events. The Rules must, of necessity, cover this multitude of situations, attempting to find wholly equitable answers to cover every eventuality. This leads them to be complex, despite the continuing efforts of rulesmakers to simplify wherever possible.

Golfers will appreciate that in a game of great tradition involving a high level of sportsmanship, strict adherence to the Rules is essential. One of the undisputed pleasures of golf lies in the comforting knowledge that all golfers around the world play the same game. Imagine the chaos that would exist if there were, as some have suggested, different rules for professional and amateur golf, if each country had its own unique code of rules, or if there were different rules for tournament play from golf played purely for the enjoyment and challenge inherent in the game.

With this background, it is with great pleasure that I introduce Golf Rules Illustrated. This publication is for golfers of all skill levels and with all levels of sophistication about the Rules. It is intended to be a user-friendly companion to the Rules of Golf to help illustrate and explain some of the most common Rules situations confronted by all golfers. Familiarity with the Rules and the examples cited will give the reader a good basic knowledge of the Rules and can help you derive even more enjoyment from the game.

Reed K. Mackenzie
Chairman, Rules of Golf Committee
United States Golf Association

Published in 2001
by Hamlyn, an imprint of Octopus Publishing Group Ltd
2–4 Heron Quays, London E14 4JP

Text copyright © 2001 United States Golf Association
Design copyright © 2001 Octopus Publishing Group Ltd

Distributed in the United States and Canada by
Sterling Publishing Co., Inc
387 Park Avenue South, New York, NY 10016-8810

ISBN 0 600 60219 2

Printed in Italy

CONTENTS

SECTION 1
ETIQUETTE

COURTESY ON THE COURSE

Safety: Prior to playing a *stroke* or making a practice swing, the player should ensure that no one is standing close by or in a position to be hit by the club, the ball or any stones, pebbles, twigs or the like which may be moved by the *stroke* or swing.

Consideration for Other Players: The player who has the *honor* should be allowed to play before his opponent or *fellow-competitor* tees his ball.

No one should move, talk or stand close to or directly behind the ball or the *hole* when a player is *addressing the ball* or making a *stroke*.

No player should play until the players in front are out of range.

Pace of Play: In the interest of all, players should play without delay.

If a player believes his ball may be *lost* outside a *water hazard* or *out of bounds,* to save time, he should play a *provisional ball.*

Players searching for a ball should signal the players behind them to pass as soon as it becomes apparent that the ball will not easily be found. They should not search for five minutes before doing so. They should not continue play until the players following them have passed and are out of range.

When the play of a hole has been completed, players should immediately leave the *putting green.*

If a match fails to keep its place on the *course* and loses more than one clear hole on the players in front, it should invite the match following to pass.

When taking a practice swing, a player should always make sure that no one is standing where they might be hit.

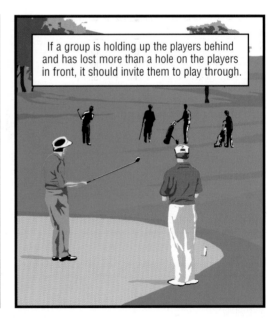

If a group is holding up the players behind and has lost more than a hole on the players in front, it should invite them to play through.

PRIORITY ON THE COURSE

In the absence of special rules, two-ball *matches* should have precedence over and be entitled to pass any three- or four-ball *match*, which should invite them through.

A single player has no standing and should give way to a *match* of any kind.

Any *match* playing a whole round is entitled to pass a *match* playing a shorter round.

CARE OF THE COURSE

Holes in Bunkers: Before leaving a *bunker*, a player should carefully fill up and smooth over all holes and footprints made by him.

Repair Divots, Ball-Marks and Damage by Spikes: A player should ensure that any divot hole made by him and any damage to the *putting green* made by a ball is carefully repaired. **On completion of the hole** by all players in the group, damage to the *putting green* caused by golf shoe spikes should be repaired.

Damage to Greens — Flagsticks, Bags, etc: Players should ensure that, when putting down bags or the *flagstick*, no damage is done to the *putting green* and that neither they nor their *caddies* damage the *hole* by standing close to it, in handling the *flagstick* or in removing the ball from the *hole*. The *flagstick* should be properly replaced in the *hole* before the players leave the *putting green*. Players should not damage the *putting green* by leaning on their putters, particularly when removing the ball from the *hole*.

Golf Carts: Local notices regulating the movement of golf carts should be strictly observed.

Damage Through Practice Swings: In taking practice swings, players should avoid causing damage to the *course*, particularly the tees, by removing divots.

Always repair divots (top right), carefully repair pitch marks on the putting green (bottom left) and smooth over footprints and other marks when leaving a bunker (bottom center). Do not lean on your putter when removing the ball from the hole (middle right).

SECTION 2
DEFINITIONS

The Definitions are placed in alphabetical order and some are also repeated at the beginning of their relevant Rule.
In the Rules themselves, defined terms which may be important to the application of a Rule are set in italics each time they appear.

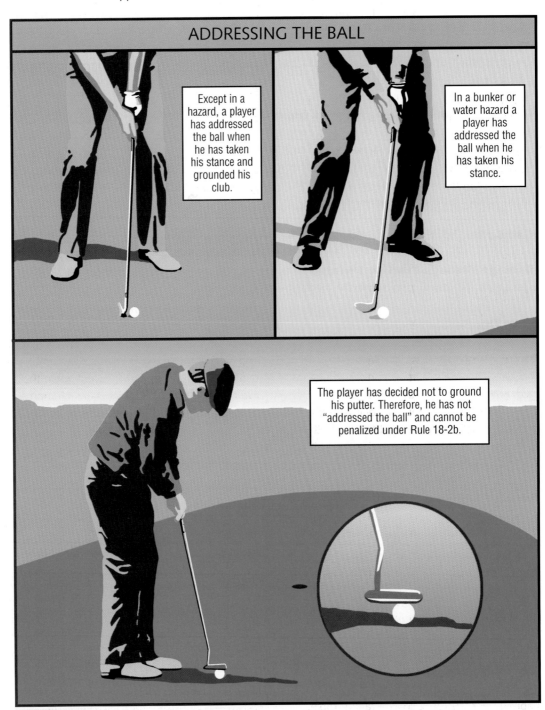

ADDRESSING THE BALL

Except in a hazard, a player has addressed the ball when he has taken his stance and grounded his club.

In a bunker or water hazard a player has addressed the ball when he has taken his stance.

The player has decided not to ground his putter. Therefore, he has not "addressed the ball" and cannot be penalized under Rule 18-2b.

Abnormal Ground Conditions: An *"abnormal ground condition"* is any *casual water, ground under repair* or hole, cast or runway on the *course* made by a *burrowing animal*, a reptile or a bird.

Addressing the Ball: A player has *"addressed the ball"* when he has taken his *stance* and has also grounded his club, except that in a *hazard* a player has *addressed the ball* when he has taken his *stance*.

Advice: *"Advice"* is any counsel or suggestion which could influence a player in determining his play, the choice of a club or the method of making a *stroke*.

Information on the *Rules* or on matters of public information, such as the position of *hazards* or the *flagstick* on the *putting green*, is not *advice*.

Ball Deemed to Move: See *"Move or Moved".*

Ball Holed: See *"Holed."*

Ball Lost: See *"Lost Ball."*

Ball in Play: A ball is *"in play"* as soon as the player has made a *stroke* on the *teeing ground*. It remains *in play* until *holed* out, except when it is *lost*, *out of bounds* or lifted, or another ball has been substituted whether or not such substitution is permitted; a ball so substituted becomes the *ball in play*.

Bunker: A *"bunker"* is a *hazard* consisting of a prepared area of ground, often a hollow, from which turf or soil has been removed and replaced with sand or the like. Grass-covered ground bordering or within a *bunker* is not part of the *bunker*. The margin of a *bunker* extends vertically downwards, but not upwards. A ball is in a *bunker* when it lies in or any part of it touches the *bunker*.

Burrowing Animal: A *"burrowing animal"* is an animal that makes a hole for habitation or shelter, such as a rabbit, mole,

CADDIE

A caddie will carry a player's clubs and offer advice on club selection, the direction of play and line for putting.

ground hog, gopher or salamander.

Note: A hole made by a non-burrowing animal, such as a dog, is not an *abnormal ground condition* unless marked or declared as *ground under repair*.

Caddie: A *"caddie"* is one who carries or handles a player's clubs during play and otherwise assists him in accordance with the *Rules*.

When one *caddie* is employed by more than one player, he is always deemed to be the *caddie* of the player whose ball is involved, and *equipment* carried by him is deemed to be that player's *equipment*, except when the *caddie* acts upon specific directions of another player, in which case he is considered to be that other player's *caddie*.

Casual Water: *"Casual water"* is any

CASUAL WATER

Casual water is an 'abnormal ground condition' and a player may take relief from such a condition under Rule 25-1.

temporary accumulation of water on the *course* which is visible before or after the player takes his *stance* and is not in a *water hazard*. Snow and natural ice, other than frost, are either *casual water* or *loose impediments*, at the option of the player. Manufactured ice is an *obstruction*. Dew and frost are not *casual water*. A ball is in *casual water* when it lies in or any part of it touches the *casual water*.

Committee: The "*Committee*" is the committee in charge of the competition or, if the matter does not arise in a competition, the committee in charge of the *course*.

Competitor: A "*competitor*" is a player in a stroke competition. A "*fellow-competitor*" is any person with whom the *competitor* plays. Neither is *partner* of the other.

In stroke play foursome and four-ball competitions, where the context so admits, the word "*competitor*" or "*fellow-competitor*" includes his *partner*.

Course: The "*course*" is the whole area within which play is permitted (see Rule 33-2).

Equipment: "*Equipment*" is anything used, worn or carried by or for the player except any ball he has played at the hole being played and any small object, such as a coin or a tee, when used to mark the position of a ball or the extent of an area in which a ball is to be dropped. *Equipment* includes a golf cart, whether or not motorized. If such a cart is shared by two or more players, the cart and everything in it are deemed to be the *equipment* of the player whose ball is involved except that, when the cart is being moved by one of the players sharing it, the cart and everything in it are deemed to be that player's *equipment*.
Note: A ball played at the hole being played is *equipment* when it has been lifted and not put back into play.

Fellow-Competitor: See "*Competitor*."

Flagstick: The "*flagstick*" is a movable straight indicator, with or without bunting or

EQUIPMENT

Equipment includes a golf cart. As it is not being moved by one of the players, the cart and everything in it are deemed to be the equipment of the player whose ball is involved.

other material attached, centered in the *hole* to show its position. It shall be circular in cross-section.

Forecaddie: A "*forecaddie*" is one who is employed by the *Committee* to indicate to players the position of balls during play. He is an *outside agency*.

Ground Under Repair: "*Ground under repair*" is any part of the *course* so marked by order of the *Committee* or so declared by its authorized representative. It includes material piled for removal and a hole made by a greenkeeper, even if not so marked.

All ground and any grass, bush, tree or other growing thing within the *ground under repair* is part of the *ground under repair*. The margin of *ground under repair* extends vertically downwards, but not upwards. Stakes and lines defining *ground under repair* are in such ground. Such stakes are *obstructions*. A ball is in *ground under repair* when it lies in or any part of it touches the *ground under repair*.
Note 1: Grass cuttings and other material left on the *course* which have been abandoned

and are not intended to be removed are not *ground under repair* unless so marked.

Note 2: The *Committee* may make a Local Rule prohibiting play from *ground under repair* or an environmentally-sensitive area which has been defined as *ground under repair*.

Hazards: A "*hazard*" is any *bunker* or *water hazard*.

Hole: The "*hole*" shall be 4 1/4 inches (108mm) in diameter and at least 4 inches (100mm) deep. If a lining is used, it shall be sunk at least 1 inch (25mm) below the *putting green* surface unless the nature of the soil makes it impracticable to do so; its outer diameter shall not exceed 4 1/4 inches (108mm).

Holed: A ball is "*holed*" when it is at rest within the circumference of the *hole* and all of it is below the level of the lip of the *hole*.

Honor: The player who is to play first from the *teeing ground* is said to have the "*honor*."

Lateral Water Hazard: A "*lateral water hazard*" is a *water hazard* or that part of a *water hazard* so situated that it is not possible or is deemed by the *Committee* to be impracticable to drop a ball behind the *water hazard* in accordance with Rule 26-1b.

That part of a *water hazard* to be played as a *lateral water hazard* should be distinctively marked. A ball is in a *lateral water hazard* when it lies in or any part of it touches the *lateral water hazard*.

Note 1: *Lateral water hazards* should be defined by red stakes or lines.

Note 2: The *Committee* may make a Local Rule prohibiting play from an environmentally-sensitive area which has been defined as a *lateral water hazard*.

Note 3: The *Committee* may define a *lateral water hazard* as a *water hazard*.

Line of Play: The "*line of play*" is the direction which the player wishes his ball to take after a *stroke*, plus a reasonable distance on either side of the intended direction. The

9

line of play extends vertically upwards from the ground, but does not extend beyond the *hole*.

Line of Putt: The "*line of putt*" is the line which the player wishes his ball to take after a *stroke* on the *putting green*. Except with respect to Rule 16-1e, the *line of putt* includes a reasonable distance on either side of the intended line. The *line of putt* does not extend beyond the *hole*.

Loose Impediments: "*Loose impediments*" are natural objects such as stones, leaves, twigs, branches and the like, dung, worms and insects and casts or heaps made by them, provided they are not fixed or growing, are not solidly embedded and do not adhere to the ball.

Sand and loose soil are *loose impediments* on the *putting green*, but not elsewhere.

Snow and natural ice, other than frost, are either *casual water* or *loose impediments*, at the option of the player. Manufactured ice is an *obstruction*.

Dew and frost are not *loose impediments*.

Lost Ball: A ball is "*lost*" if:

a. It is not found or identified as his by the player within five minutes after the player's *side* or his or their *caddies* have begun to search for it; or

b. The player has put another ball into play under the *Rules*, even though he may not have searched for the original ball; or

c. The player has played any *stroke* with a *provisional ball* from the place where the original ball is likely to be or from a point nearer the *hole* than that place, whereupon the *provisional ball* becomes the *ball in play*.

Time spent in playing a *wrong ball* is not counted in the five-minute period allowed for search.

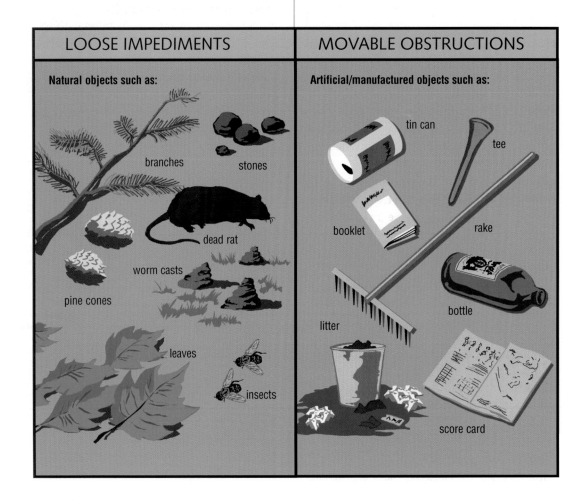

LOOSE IMPEDIMENTS	MOVABLE OBSTRUCTIONS
Natural objects such as:	**Artificial/manufactured objects such as:**

LOOSE IMPEDIMENTS — Natural objects such as: branches, stones, pine cones, worm casts, dead rat, leaves, insects

MOVABLE OBSTRUCTIONS — Artificial/manufactured objects such as: tin can, tee, booklet, rake, bottle, litter, score card

BALL DEEMED TO MOVE

This ball is deemed not to have 'moved' because, having left its original position, it rolled back into it again.

This ball is deemed to have 'moved' because it has left its original position and come to rest in another place; the fact that it has moved vertically, rather than laterally, is irrelevant.

Marker: A "*marker*" is one who is appointed by the *Committee* to record a *competitor*'s score in stroke play. He may be a *fellow-competitor*. He is not a *referee*.

Matches: See "*Sides* and *Matches.*"

Move or Moved: A ball is deemed to have "*moved*" if it leaves its position and comes to rest in any other place.

Nearest Point of Relief: The "*nearest point of relief*" is the reference point for taking relief without penalty from interference by an immovable *obstruction* (Rule 24-2), an *abnormal ground condition* (Rule 25-1) or a *wrong putting green* (Rule 25-3).

It is the point on the *course* nearest to where the ball lies, which is not nearer the *hole* and at which, if the ball were so positioned, no interference (as defined) would exist.

Note: The player should determine his *nearest point of relief* by using the club with which he expects to play his next *stroke* to simulate the *address* position and swing for such *stroke*.

Observer: An "*observer*" is one who is appointed by the *Committee* to assist a *referee* to decide questions of fact and to report to him any breach of a *Rule*. An *observer* should not attend the *flagstick*, stand at or mark the position of the *hole*, or lift the ball or mark its position.

Obstructions: An "*obstruction*" is anything artificial, including the artificial surfaces and sides of roads and paths and manufactured ice, except:

a. Objects defining *out of bounds*, such as walls, fences, stakes and railings;

b. Any part of an immovable artificial object which is *out of bounds*; and

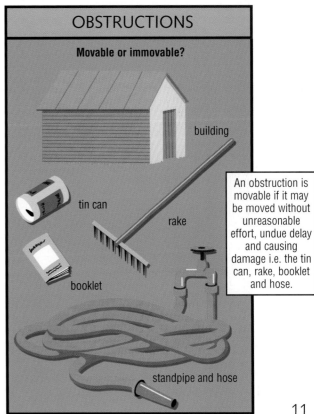

OBSTRUCTIONS

Movable or immovable?

building

tin can

rake

booklet

standpipe and hose

An obstruction is movable if it may be moved without unreasonable effort, undue delay and causing damage i.e. the tin can, rake, booklet and hose.

c. Any construction declared by the *Committee* to be an integral part of the *course*.

An *obstruction* is a movable *obstruction* if it may be moved without unreasonable effort, without unduly delaying play and without causing damage. Otherwise it is an immovable *obstruction*.

Note: The *Committee* may make a Local Rule declaring a movable *obstruction* to be an immovable *obstruction*.

Out of Bounds: "*Out of bounds*" is beyond the boundaries of the *course* or any part of the *course* so marked by the *Committee*.

When *out of bounds* is defined by reference to stakes or a fence or as being beyond stakes or a fence, the *out of bounds* line is determined by the nearest inside points of the stakes or fence posts at ground level excluding angled supports.

Objects defining *out of bounds* such as walls, fences, stakes and railings, are not *obstructions* and are deemed to be fixed.

When *out of bounds* is defined by a line on the ground, the line itself is *out of bounds*.

The *out of bounds* line extends vertically upwards and downwards.

A ball is *out of bounds* when all of it lies *out of bounds*.

A player may stand *out of bounds* to play a ball lying within bounds.

Outside Agency: An "*outside agency*" is any agency not part of the match or, in stroke play, not part of the *competitor*'s *side*, and includes a *referee*, a *marker*, an *observer* and a *forecaddie*. Neither wind nor water is an *outside agency*.

Partner: A "*partner*" is a player associated with another player on the same *side*.
In a threesome, foursome, best-ball or four-ball match, where the context so admits, the word "player" includes his *partner* or *partners*.

Penalty Stroke: A "*penalty stroke*" is one added to the score of a player or *side* under certain Rules. In a threesome or foursome, *penalty strokes* do not affect the order of play.

Provisional Ball: A "*provisional ball*" is a ball played under Rule 27-2 for a ball which may be *lost* outside a *water hazard* or may be *out of bounds*.

Putting Green: The "*putting green*" is all ground of the hole being played which is specially prepared for putting or otherwise defined as such by the *Committee*. A ball is on the *putting green* when any part of it touches the *putting green*.

Referee: A "*referee*" is one who is appointed by the *Committee* to accompany players to decide questions of fact and apply the *Rules*. He shall act on any breach of a Rule which he observes or is reported to him.

A *referee* should not attend the *flagstick*, stand at or mark the position of the *hole*, or lift the ball or mark its position.

PARTNER

A partner is a player associated with another player on the same side.

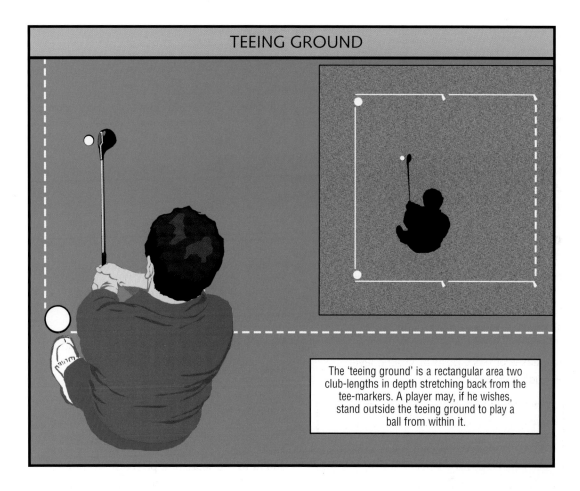

TEEING GROUND

The 'teeing ground' is a rectangular area two club-lengths in depth stretching back from the tee-markers. A player may, if he wishes, stand outside the teeing ground to play a ball from within it.

Rub of the Green: A "*rub of the green*" occurs when a ball in motion is accidentally deflected or stopped by any *outside agency* (see Rule 19-1).

Rule: The term "Rule" includes:
a. The Rules of Golf;
b. Any Local Rules made by the *Committee* under Rule 33-8a and Appendix I; and
c. The specifications on clubs and the ball in Appendices II and III.

Sides and Matches:
Side: A player, or two or more players who are *partners*.
Single: A match in which one plays against another.
Threesome: A match in which one plays against two, and each *side* plays one ball.
Foursome: A match in which two play against two, and each *side* plays one ball.
Three-Ball: A match play competition in which three play against one another, each playing his own ball. Each player is playing two distinct *matches*.
Best-Ball: A match in which one plays against the better ball of two or the best ball of three players.
Four-Ball: A match in which two play their better ball against the better ball of two other players.

Stance: Taking the "*stance*" consists in a player placing his feet in position for and preparatory to making a *stroke*.

Stipulated Round: The "*stipulated round*" consists of playing the holes of the *course* in their correct sequence unless otherwise authorized by the *Committee*. The number of holes in a *stipulated round* is 18 unless a smaller number is authorized by the *Committee*. As to extension of *stipulated round* in match play, see Rule 2-3.

DEFINITION OF A STROKE

At this point, as the player has not started his downswing, he has not begun his stroke. Once the player begins his downswing he is considered to have made a stroke, unless he checks his downswing voluntarily.

Stroke: A "*stroke*" is the forward movement of the club made with the intention of fairly striking at and moving the ball, but if a player checks his downswing voluntarily before the clubhead reaches the ball he is deemed not to have made a *stroke*.

Teeing Ground: The "*teeing ground*" is the starting place for the hole to be played. It is a rectangular area two club-lengths in depth, the front and the sides of which are defined by the outside limits of two tee-markers. A ball is outside the *teeing ground* when all of it lies outside the *teeing ground*.

Through the Green: "*Through the green*" is the whole area of the *course* except:
a. The *teeing ground* and *putting green* of the hole being played; and
b. All *hazards* on the *course*.

Water Hazard: A "*water hazard*" is any sea, lake, pond, river, ditch, surface drainage ditch or other open water course (whether or not containing water) and anything of a similar nature.

All ground or water within the margin of a *water hazard* is part of the *water hazard*. The margin of a *water hazard* extends vertically upwards and downwards. Stakes and lines defining the margins of *water hazards* are in the *hazards*. Such stakes are *obstructions*. A ball is in a *water hazard* when it lies in or any part of it touches the *water hazard*.

Note 1: *Water hazards* (other than *lateral water hazards*) should be defined by yellow stakes or lines.

Note 2: The *Committee* may make a Local Rule prohibiting play from an environmentally-sensitive area which has been defined as a *water hazard*.

Wrong Ball: A "*wrong ball*" is any ball other than the player's:
a. *Ball in play*,
b. *Provisional ball*, or
c. Second ball played under Rule 3-3 or Rule 20-7b in stroke play.

Note: *Ball in play* includes a ball substituted for the *ball in play* whether or not such substitution is permitted.

Wrong Putting Green: A "*wrong putting green*" is any *putting green* other than that of the hole being played. Unless otherwise prescribed by the *Committee,* this term includes a practice *putting green* or pitching green on the *course*.

SECTION 3
THE RULES OF PLAY

RULE **1** | ## THE GAME

See **incident** involving Rule 1-1 on page 16

1-1 GENERAL
The Game of Golf consists in playing a ball from the *teeing ground* into the *hole* by a *stroke* or successive *strokes* in accordance with the *Rules*.

1-2 EXERTING INFLUENCE ON BALL
No player or *caddie* shall take any action to influence the position or the movement of a ball except in accordance with the *Rules*.
(Removal of movable *obstruction* — see Rule 24-1.)
PENALTY FOR BREACH OF RULE 1-2: *Match Play — Loss of hole; Stroke play — Two strokes.*
Note: In the case of a serious breach of Rule 1-2, the *Committee* may impose a penalty of disqualification.

1-3 AGREEMENT TO WAIVE RULES
Players shall not agree to exclude the operation of any *Rule* or to waive any penalty incurred.
PENALTY FOR BREACH OF RULE 1-3: *Match play — Disqualification of both sides; Stroke play — Disqualification of competitors concerned.*
(Agreeing to play out of turn in stroke play — see Rule 10-2c.)

MATCH PLAY: AGREEMENT TO CONSIDER HOLE HALVED

An agreement to halve a hole being played is not an agreement to waive the Rules.

EQUITY – SOME EXAMPLES

Ball comes to rest near bee's nest. Player is entitled to relief –. Decision 1-4/10

Ball adheres to face of club after stroke. Player drops ball on spot where club was when ball stuck to it – Decision 1-4/2

Distractions are common place, but some problems less so. Wildlife needs to be protected and sometimes so does the golfer.

Bird's nest interferes with stroke. Player is entitled to relief– Decision 1-4/9

Ball comes to rest near snake. Player is entitled to relief – Decision 1-4/10

1-4 POINTS NOT COVERED BY RULES

If any point in dispute is not covered by the *Rules,* the decision shall be made in accordance with equity.

RULE 1 INCIDENT

The 1954 U.S. Open was the fourth time the national championship had been played at Baltusrol Golf Club, it was the first time the Lower Course had been used, the first time the championship had been televised nationwide and the first time every hole was roped from tee to green to control spectators.

As a child, Ed Furgol had fallen from a set of parallel bars, crippling his left arm. Three corrective surgeries had left the arm shortened and unable to be straightened beyond 45 degrees. The New York Mills native had tenaciously developed a unique style to compensate for his handicap. When his adapted swing worked, the results were stunning, as his first three rounds of 71-70-71 at Baltusrol attested. But when it failed, the resulting hook could spell disaster.

After a 20-minute wait on the tee of the par-5 final hole, Furgol hooked his drive into the trees that border the left side. The dense woodland blocked a play toward the green. The only line back to the

18th fairway was so acute that such a play would have resulted in Furgol not being able to reach the green with his third shot.

In a nearly opposite direction, Furgol saw an opening onto the 18th fairway of Baltusrol's Upper Course, which runs parallel to the last fairway of the Lower Course. The fertile imagination that had envisioned the golf swing that had brought Furgol to this point of contention had no problem envisioning a line via the Upper Course to the final green of the Lower.

The game of golf consists of playing a ball from the teeing ground into the hole, as stated by Rule 1. How a player negotiates hazards and obstacles along the course is part of each player's creative test as long as such decisions are permitted under the Rules. Playing onto an adjacent course is permissible as long as it is not out of bounds. Rules officials confirmed this fact when Furgol inquired before playing his second stroke.

Furgol punched his second shot through the trees and onto the 18th fairway of the Upper Course. From there, he pitched onto the 18th green of the Lower Course and two putted to win the U.S. Open, $6,000 in prize money and, as a result, the 1954 PGA Player of the Year Award.

RULE  # MATCH PLAY

2-1 WINNER OF HOLE; RECKONING OF HOLES

In match play the game is played by holes.

Except as otherwise provided in the *Rules*, a hole is won by the *side* which *holes* its ball in the fewer *strokes*. In a handicap match the lower net score wins the hole.

The reckoning of holes is kept by the terms: so many "holes up" or "all square," and so many "to play."

A *side* is "dormie" when it is as many holes up as there are holes remaining to be played.

2-2 HALVED HOLE

A hole is halved if each *side holes* out in the same number of *strokes*.

When a player has *holed* out and his opponent has been left with a *stroke* for the half, if the player thereafter incurs a penalty, the hole is halved.

2-3 WINNER OF MATCH

A match (which consists of a *stipulated round*, unless otherwise decreed by the *Committee*) is won by the *side* which is leading by a number of holes greater than the number of holes remaining to be played.

The *Committee* may, for the purpose of settling a tie, extend the *stipulated round* to as many holes as are required for a match to be won.

See **incident** involving Rule 2-4 on page 19

2-4 CONCESSION OF NEXT STROKE, HOLE OR MATCH

When the opponent's ball is at rest or is deemed to be at rest under Rule 16-2, the player may concede the opponent to have *holed* out with his next *stroke* and the ball may be removed by either *side* with a club or otherwise.

A player may concede a hole or a match at any time prior to the conclusion of the hole or the match.

Concession of a *stroke*, hole or match may not be declined or withdrawn.

2-5 CLAIMS

In match play, if a doubt or dispute arises between the players and no duly authorized representative of the *Committee* is available within a reasonable time, the players shall continue the match without delay. Any claim, if it is to be considered by the *Committee*, must be made before any player in the match plays from the next *teeing ground* or, in the case of the last hole of the match, before all players in the match leave the *putting green*.

No later claim shall be considered unless it is based on facts previously unknown to the player making the claim and the player making the claim had been given wrong information (Rules 6-2a and 9) by an opponent. In any case, no later claim shall be considered after the result of the match has been officially announced, unless the *Committee* is satisfied that the opponent knew he was giving wrong information.

2-6 GENERAL PENALTY

The penalty for a breach of a *Rule* in match play is loss of hole except when otherwise provided.

RULE 2 INCIDENT

Jack Nicklaus' concession of Tony Jacklin's putt on the final hole during the final match of the 1969 Ryder Cup resulted in this match play event's first tie, and is hailed as one of golf's finest acts of sportsmanship.

Going into the final day's competition at Royal Birkdale Golf Club in Southport, England, the United States and Great Britain were even at eight points apiece. That morning's singles matches resulted in a two-point lead by the British, which was reciprocated by the U.S. in the afternoon to leave the matches tied at 15 1/2 with only the final match of Nicklaus and Jacklin still on the course. Eighteen of the 32 Ryder Cup matches went to the final hole that year, and it was there that the three-day competition would be ultimately decided.

Nicklaus had the upper hand as Jacklin had fallen behind on the back nine. As the reigning British Open champion, Jacklin would not relent. Indeed, he eagled the 17th to go all square with Nicklaus.

As the defending champions after their victory in 1967 at Champions Golf Club in Houston, the U.S. team needed only a tie at the last hole to tie the overall competition, which would ensure that the cup remained with the U.S. team.

At the par-5 18th, Jacklin missed his putt for birdie. Nicklaus holed his four-footer for par. Jacklin was left with a short putt to tie Nicklaus. If he holed the putt, it would be the first time the Ryder Cup had ended in a tie. A miss by Jacklin would result in an outright win by the Americans.

Before Jacklin could putt, Nicklaus picked up Jacklin's marker, conceding the Englishman's putt and insuring a tie. "I don't think you would have missed that Tony," Nicklaus reportedly said, "but under these circumstances I'd never give you the opportunity."

"The length of the putt has varied after thirty years," Jacklin has stated to reporters. "It's been as long as four feet. But my recollection is twenty inches. Of course, I could have missed it; there are no guarantees in golf, especially in the crucible of the Ryder Cup, but I believe I would have made it. But Jack saw the big picture, two months before I had become the first British player in 18 years to win the British Open, so there was very much a pro-British fervor at the Ryder Cup in England that year. Jack saw that the putt on the last hole in 1969 meant a heck of a lot more to the Ryder Cup than who won or lost that particular match. It was a great moment."

RULE | ## STROKE PLAY

3-1 WINNER
The *competitor* who plays the *stipulated round* or rounds in the fewest strokes is the winner.

3-2 FAILURE TO HOLE OUT
If a *competitor* fails to *hole* out at any hole and does not correct his mistake before he plays a *stroke* from the next *teeing ground* or, in the case of the last hole of the round, before he leaves the *putting green*, **he shall be disqualified**.

3-3 DOUBT AS TO PROCEDURE
a Procedure
In stroke play only, when during play of a hole a *competitor* is doubtful of his rights or procedure, he may, without penalty, play a second ball. After the situation which caused the doubt has arisen, the *competitor* should, before taking further action, announce to his *marker* or a *fellow-competitor* his decision to invoke this Rule and the ball with which he will score if the *Rules* permit.

The *competitor* shall report the facts to the *Committee* before returning his score card unless he scores the same with both balls; if he fails to do so, **he shall be disqualified**.

b Determination of Score for Hole
If the *Rules* allow the procedure selected in advance by the *competitor*, the score with the ball selected shall be his score for the hole.

If the *competitor* fails to announce in advance his decision to invoke this Rule or his selection, the score with the original ball or, if the original ball is not one of the balls being played, the first ball put into play shall count if the *Rules* allow the procedure adopted for such ball.

See **background** concerning Rule 3 on page 21

Note 1: If a *competitor* plays a second ball, *penalty strokes* incurred solely by playing the ball ruled not to count and *strokes* subsequently taken with that ball shall be disregarded.

Note 2: A second ball played under Rule 3-3 is not a *provisional ball* under Rule 27-2.

3-4 REFUSAL TO COMPLY WITH A RULE

If a *competitor* refuses to comply with a *Rule* affecting the rights of another *competitor*, **he shall be disqualified**.

3-5 GENERAL PENALTY

The penalty for a breach of a *Rule* in stroke play is two strokes except when otherwise provided.

RULE 3 BACKGROUND

Match play came first to golf. One played against another, one hole and one match at a time. Then, sometimes, two might play against two, or maybe two played against one. Whatever the configuration, the match being played was that match's total universe until it was decided. Putts, holes and matches could be conceded. If you lay 2 beside the hole and your opponent lay 9, he could give you the hole and you walked to the next tee. If your opponents were too ill to play, they could give you the match.

By the mid-18th century, when golf clubs were being formed in Scotland, their members desired a different form of competition in which the total number of strokes taken to play a course would be counted. On May 9, 1759 the Society of St. Andrews Golfers resolved "... whoever puts in the Ball at the fewest Strokes Over the Field, being 22 Holes, Shall be Declared and Sustain Victor." The victor was often awarded a medal from which the term "medal play" finds its origin.

During stroke play a few things, which had been decided by loss of hole in match play, needed more precise direction. These Rules remain today. For instance, all balls must be holed out in stroke play. Without such a stipulation, a player's round is incomplete and the score incomparable to those who have holed out. The player now, as then, is disqualified if he does not hole out, because he has not completed the course.

To insure that everyone plays the same course, tee-markers take on added importance in stroke play. Beginning a hole from outside the markers results in a two-stroke penalty and a ball must be played from within their boundaries. Just as all players must end in the same place, they must also begin in the same place. Failure to correct an error of this type also results in disqualification.

Another important distinction is the method used when doubt arises about how to proceed. Rule 3-3 allows those competing in stroke play to play a second ball. The player must announce ahead of time his intent to play a second ball and which ball he wishes to use should the Rules allow it. In match play, playing a second ball is not permitted. Rather, the player must make a specific claim if he objects to an action taken by his opponent before anyone plays from the next teeing ground.

Because the total number of strokes determines the winner in stroke play, the score card becomes each player's testament to what he has accomplished on the course, and a marker must attest it. Errors in scorekeeping cannot be tolerated when the best score is what determines the winner. Thus, a score for a hole that is recorded higher than actually taken can be included because it would not create an advantage, but a lower score must result in disqualification because it would create one.

The responsibility for violations in both forms of play rests with the players themselves. However, a loss of hole penalty in match play can be assessed and the match continued. While there are 15 one-stroke penalties that apply to both forms of play, the general penalty in stroke play is two strokes and play continues. However, a stroke play violation that results in a serious inequity between a player's procedure and that of the entire field must logically result in disqualification.

CLUBS AND THE BALL

The United States Golf Association reserves the right to change the *Rules* and make and change the interpretations relating to clubs, balls and other implements at any time.

RULE

CLUBS

A player in doubt as to the conformity of a club should consult the United States Golf Association.

A manufacturer should submit to the United States Golf Association a sample of a club which is to be manufactured for a ruling as to whether the club conforms with the *Rules*. If a manufacturer fails to submit a sample before manufacturing and/or marketing the club, the manufacturer assumes the risk of a ruling that the club does not conform with the *Rules*. Any sample submitted to the United States Golf Association will become its property for reference purposes.

4-1 FORM AND MAKE OF CLUBS
a General
The player's clubs shall conform with this Rule and the provisions, specifications and interpretations set forth in Appendix II.

b Wear and Alteration
A club which conforms with the *Rules* when new is deemed to conform after wear through normal use. Any part of a club which has been purposely altered is regarded as new and must, in its altered state, conform with the *Rules*.

4-2 PLAYING CHARACTERISTICS CHANGED AND FOREIGN MATERIAL
a Playing Characteristics Changed
During a *stipulated round,* the playing characteristics of a club shall not be purposely changed by adjustment or by any other means.

b Foreign Material
Foreign material must not be applied to the club face for the purpose of influencing the movement of the ball.

PENALTY FOR BREACH OF RULE 4-1 or -2: *Disqualification.*

4-3 DAMAGED CLUBS: REPAIR AND REPLACEMENT
a Damage in Normal Course of Play
If, during a *stipulated round*, a player's club is damaged in the normal course of play, he may:
(i)   use the club in its damaged state for the remainder of the *stipulated round*; or
(ii) without unduly delaying play, repair it or have it repaired; or
(iii) **as an additional option available only if the club is unfit for play,**

23

replace the damaged club with any club. The replacement of a club must not unduly delay play and must not be made by borrowing any club selected for play by any other person playing on the *course*.

PENALTY FOR BREACH OF RULE 4-3a: *See Penalty Statement for Rule 4-4a or b.*

Note: A club is unfit for play if it is substantially damaged, e.g., the shaft breaks into pieces or the clubhead becomes loose, detached or significantly deformed. A club is not unfit for play solely because the shaft is bent, the club's lie or loft has been altered or the clubhead is scratched.

See **incident** involving Rule 4-3b on page 26

b Damage Other Than in Normal Course of Play

If, during a *stipulated round*, a player's club is damaged other than in the normal course of play rendering it non-conforming or changing its playing characteristics, the club shall not subsequently be used or replaced during the round.

c Damage Prior to Round

A player may use a club damaged prior to a round provided the club, in its damaged state, conforms with the *Rules*.

Damage to a club which occurred prior to a round may be repaired during the round, provided the playing characteristics are not changed and play is not unduly delayed.

PENALTY FOR BREACH OF RULE 4-3b or c: *Disqualification.*

(Undue delay – see Rule 6-7.)

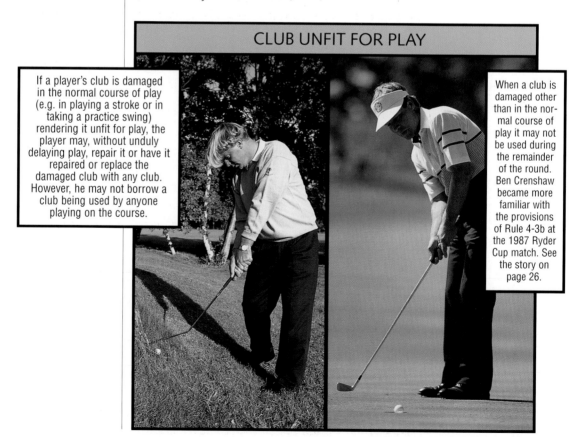

CLUB UNFIT FOR PLAY

If a player's club is damaged in the normal course of play (e.g. in playing a stroke or in taking a practice swing) rendering it unfit for play, the player may, without unduly delaying play, repair it or have it repaired or replace the damaged club with any club. However, he may not borrow a club being used by anyone playing on the course.

When a club is damaged other than in the normal course of play it may not be used during the remainder of the round. Ben Crenshaw became more familiar with the provisions of Rule 4-3b at the 1987 Ryder Cup match. See the story on page 26.

BREACH OF 14-CLUB RULE IN MATCH PLAY

4-4 MAXIMUM OF FOURTEEN CLUBS
a Selection and Addition of Clubs
The player shall start a *stipulated round* with not more than fourteen clubs. He is limited to the clubs thus selected for that round except that, if he started with fewer than fourteen clubs, he may add any number provided his total number does not exceed fourteen.

The addition of a club or clubs must not unduly delay play (Rule 6-7) and must not be made by borrowing any club selected for play by any other person playing on the *course*.

b Partners May Share Clubs
Partners may share clubs, provided that the total number of clubs carried by the *partners* so sharing does not exceed fourteen.

PENALTY FOR BREACH OF RULE 4-4a or b, REGARDLESS OF NUMBER OF EXCESS CLUBS CARRIED: *Match play* — At the conclusion of the hole at which the breach is discovered, the state of the match shall be adjusted by deducting one hole for each hole at which a breach occurred. Maximum deduction per round: two holes.

Stroke play — Two strokes for each hole at which any breach occurred; maximum penalty per round: four strokes.

Bogey and par competitions — Penalties as in match play.

Stableford competitions — see Note to Rule 32-1b.

c Excess Club Declared Out of Play
Any club carried or used in breach of this Rule shall be declared out of play by the player immediately upon discovery that a breach has occurred and thereafter shall not be used by the player during the round.

PENALTY FOR BREACH OF RULE 4-4c: *Disqualification.*

RULE 4 INCIDENT

As Ben Crenshaw walked down a gravel pathway at Muirfield Village during the 1987 Ryder Cup, he was lightly bouncing his putter along the ground in time with his steps when the club's shaft broke.

It was the third and final day of the competition. Crenshaw was competing against Eamonn Darcy in the singles. The American team had finished the previous day trailing the European team by five points. The matches in front of Crenshaw and Darcy were tilting in favor of the Americans, and those behind could go either way. To avoid the first defeat of a U.S. Ryder Cup team on American soil, every point had become crucial.

It did not matter that Crenshaw's putter was damaged without anger or malice. Because the club was damaged "other than in the normal course of play," America's best putter would now suffer the consequences of Rule 4. He could not use the putter, repair it or replace it.

For the second nine holes, Crenshaw used various clubs for putting — sometimes a 1-iron, sometimes a sand wedge. The Texan's misfortune, coupled with the intensity of the Ryder Cup singles competition, seemed to provide extraordinary focus and he continued to putt well, especially well since he didn't have a putter. The match went to the 18th hole where Darcy won 1 up.

With a final score of 15-13, the European team won the Ryder Cup for the first time on American soil. Had Crenshaw won his match, the competition would have ended in a tie. Had that been the case, the Europeans, as defending champions, would still have retained the cup.

RULE | # THE BALL

5-1 GENERAL

The ball the player uses shall conform to requirements specified in Appendix III.
Note: The *Committee* may require, in the conditions of a competition (Rule 33-1), that the ball the player uses must be named on the current List of Conforming Golf Balls issued by the United States Golf Association.

5-2 FOREIGN MATERIAL

Foreign material must not be applied to a ball for the purpose of changing its playing characteristics.
PENALTY FOR BREACH OF RULE 5-1 or -2: *Disqualification.*

5-3 BALL UNFIT FOR PLAY

See **incident** involving Rule 5-3 on page 28

A ball is unfit for play if it is visibly cut, cracked or out of shape. A ball is not unfit for play solely because mud or other materials adhere to it, its surface is scratched or scraped or its paint is damaged or discolored.

If a player has reason to believe his ball has become unfit for play during the play of the hole being played, he may during the play of such hole lift his ball without penalty to determine whether it is unfit.

BALL UNFIT FOR PLAY

The player must give his opponent, marker or fellow-competitor an opportunity to inspect a ball that a player believes is unfit for play. In some cases, a referee may be asked to participate in this process. See the story on page 28 involving Tiger Woods at the 1994 U.S. Amateur.

Before lifting the ball, the player must announce his intention to his opponent in match play or his *marker* or a *fellow-competitor* in stroke play and mark the position of the ball. He may then lift and examine the ball without cleaning it and must give his opponent, *marker* or *fellow-competitor* an opportunity to examine the ball.

If he fails to comply with this procedure, **he shall incur a penalty of one stroke**.

If it is determined that the ball has become unfit for play during play of the hole being played, the player may substitute another ball, placing it on the spot where the original ball lay. Otherwise, the original ball shall be replaced.

If a ball breaks into pieces as a result of a *stroke*, the stroke shall be cancelled and the player shall play a ball without penalty as nearly as possible at the spot from which the original ball was played (see Rule 20-5).

*PENALTY FOR BREACH OF RULE 5-3: *Match play — Loss of hole; Stroke play — Two strokes.*

If a player incurs the general penalty for breach of Rule 5-3, no additional penalty under the Rule shall be applied.

Note: If the opponent, *marker* or *fellow-competitor* wishes to dispute a claim of unfitness, he must do so before the player plays another ball. (Cleaning ball lifted from *putting green* or under any other Rule — see Rule 21.)

RULE 5 INCIDENT

During the final match of the 1994 U.S. Amateur Championship, Tiger Woods learned that one of the very specific instances in the Rules when a referee is not to be involved, except as a last resort, is in determining whether or not a ball is unfit for play during the play of a hole.

One down to Trip Kuehne with five holes left in the 36-hole match, Woods' drive from the 14th tee of the TPC at Sawgrass struck a cart path and a media vehicle before finally coming to rest. The lie and angle to the green were good enough for him to reach the green with his second shot, which he did.

Once on the putting green, Woods marked and lifted his ball. It was then that he questioned whether or not his ball had been rendered unfit for play by virtue of its striking the path and the vehicle. Woods' inquiry was directed to the referee who was walking with the match. The referee responded that Woods would have to make that determination after giving his opponent an opportunity to examine the ball.

After inspecting Woods' ball, Kuehne said he was unsure whether or not it was unfit. This sent Woods back to the referee for an opinion.

While Decision 5-3/7 permits a referee to make such a call, it also states that every effort should be made to have the opponent, marker or fellow-competitor fulfill his responsibilities under Rule 5-3. In this situation, Woods' opponent was not able to fulfill his responsibilities because he did not know if a ball was unfit simply because it was scarred from bouncing off of a cart path.

With Kuehne unsure and Woods entitled to a ruling, the referee determined that a new ball could not be substituted. Rule 5-3 is specific in stating that a ball is not unfit when its surface is scratched or scraped or its paint is damaged or discolored.

Woods halved the hole with the scraped ball. After birdies at the 16th and 17th, Woods was 1 up. Woods' par, conceded by Kuehne at the 18th, gave Woods a 2 up victory and the first of his three consecutive U.S. Amateur titles.

RULE THE PLAYER

DEFINITION

A *"marker"* is one who is appointed by the *Committee* to record a *competitor's* score in stroke play. He may be a *fellow-competitor*. He is not a *referee*.

6-1 RULES; CONDITIONS OF COMPETITION

The player is responsible for knowing the *Rules* and the conditions under which the competition is to be played (Rule 33-1).

6-2 HANDICAP
a Match Play

Before starting a match in a handicap competition, the players should determine from one another their respective handicaps. If a player begins the match having declared a higher handicap which would affect the number of strokes given or received, **he shall be disqualified**; otherwise, the player shall play off the declared handicap.

b Stroke Play

In any round of a handicap competition, the competitor shall ensure that his handicap is recorded on his score card before it is returned to the Committee. If no handicap is recorded on his score card before it is returned, or if the recorded handicap is higher than that to which he is entitled and this affects the number of strokes received, **he shall be disqualified** from the handicap competition; otherwise, the score shall stand.
Note: It is the player's responsibility to know the holes at which handicap strokes are to be given or received.

6-3 TIME OF STARTING AND GROUPS
a Time of Starting

The player shall start at the time laid down by the *Committee*.

b Groups

In stroke play, the *competitor* shall remain throughout the round in the group arranged by the *Committee* unless the *Committee* authorizes or ratifies a change.

PENALTY FOR BREACH OF RULE 6-3: *Disqualification.*

29

(Best-ball and four-ball play — see Rules 30-3a and 31-2.)

Note: The *Committee* may provide in the conditions of a competition (Rule 33-1) that, if the player arrives at his starting point, ready to play, within five minutes after his starting time, in the absence of circumstances which warrant waiving the penalty of disqualification as provided in Rule 33-7, the penalty for failure to start on time is **loss of the first hole in match play or two strokes at the first hole in stroke play** instead of disqualification.

6-4 CADDIE

The player may have only one *caddie* at any one time, **under penalty of disqualification**.

For any breach of a *Rule* by his *caddie*, the player incurs the applicable penalty.

6-5 BALL

The responsibility for playing the proper ball rests with the player. Each player should put an identification mark on his ball.

6-6 SCORING IN STROKE PLAY
a Recording Scores

After each hole the *marker* should check the score with the *competitor* and record it. On completion of the round the *marker* shall sign the card and hand it to the *competitor*. If more than one *marker* records the scores, each shall sign for the part for which he is responsible.

See **incident** involving Rule 6-6b on page 35

b Signing and Returning Card

After completion of the round, the competitor should check his score for each hole and settle any doubtful points with the Committee. He shall ensure that the marker has signed the card, countersign the card himself and return it to the Committee as soon as possible.

PENALTY FOR BREACH OF RULE 6-6b: *Disqualification.*

The responsibility for playing the proper ball rests with the player. PGA Tour player Duffy Waldorf has his wife and children assist him in putting identification marks on his golf balls.

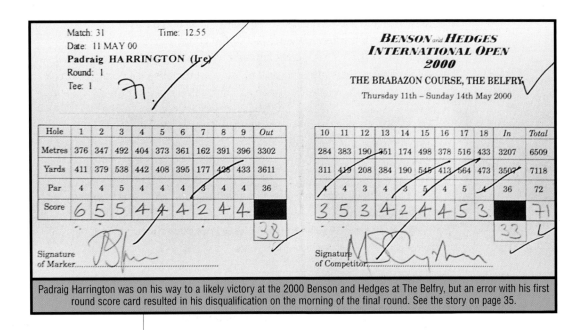

Hole	1	2	3	4	5	6	7	8	9	Out	10	11	12	13	14	15	16	17	18	In	Total
Metres	376	347	492	404	373	361	162	391	396	3302	284	383	190	351	174	498	378	516	433	3207	6509
Yards	411	379	538	442	408	395	177	428	433	3611	311	419	208	384	190	545	413	564	473	3507	7118
Par	4	4	5	4	4	4	3	4	4	36	4	4	3	4	3	5	4	5	4	36	72
Score	6	5	5	4	4	4	2	4	4	38	3	5	3	4	2	4	4	5	3	33	71

Match: 31   Time: 12.55
Date: 11 MAY 00
Padraig HARRINGTON (Ire)
Round: 1
Tee: 1

BENSON and HEDGES
INTERNATIONAL OPEN
2000
THE BRABAZON COURSE, THE BELFRY
Thursday 11th – Sunday 14th May 2000

Signature of Marker.....................

Signature of Competitor.....................

Padraig Harrington was on his way to a likely victory at the 2000 Benson and Hedges at The Belfry, but an error with his first round score card resulted in his disqualification on the morning of the final round. See the story on page 35.

c Alteration of Card

No alteration may be made on a card after the *competitor* has returned it to the *Committee*.

d Wrong Score for Hole

See **incident** involving Rule 6-6d on page 35

The *competitor* is responsible for the correctness of the score recorded for each hole on his card. If he returns a score for any hole lower than actually taken, **he shall be disqualified**. If he returns a score for any hole higher than actually taken, the score as returned shall stand.

Note 1: The *Committee* is responsible for the addition of scores and application of the handicap recorded on the card — see Rule 33-5.

Note 2: In four-ball stroke play, see also Rule 31-4 and -7a.

6-7 UNDUE DELAY; SLOW PLAY

The player shall play without undue delay and in accordance with any pace of play guidelines which may be laid down by the *Committee*. Between completion of a hole and playing from the next *teeing ground*, the player shall not unduly delay play.

PENALTY FOR BREACH OF RULE 6-7: *Match play — Loss of hole; Stroke play — Two strokes.*

Bogey and par competitions — See Note 2 to Rule 32-1a.

Stableford competitions — See Note 2 to Rule 32-1b.

For subsequent offence — Disqualification.

Note 1: If the player unduly delays play between holes, he is delaying the play of the next hole and, except for bogey, par and stableford competitions (see Rule 32), the penalty applies to that hole.

Note 2: For the purpose of preventing slow play, the *Committee* may, in the conditions of a competition (Rule 33-1), lay down pace of play guidelines including maximum periods of time allowed to complete a *stipulated round*, a hole or a *stroke*.

SCORING IN STROKE PLAY

COMPETITION _SPRING STROKE PLAY_   DATE _14 . 6 . 95_

PLAYER _D. BROWN_   HANDICAP _10_   Game No _21_

Hole	Yards	Par	Stroke Index	Score	W L H O POINTS	Mar Score	Hole	Yards	Par	Stroke Index	Score	W L H O POINTS	Mar Score
1	312	4	17	5		6	10	369	4	12	6 5 (c)		
2	446	4	1	4		4	11	433	4	2	3		
3	310	4	13	4		3	12	361	4	14	4		
4	370	4	9	5	(b)	5	13	415	4	6	5		
5	478	5	3	6			14	155	3	16	6		
8 7	429	4	11	4			15	338	4	8	5		
7 6	385	4	5	3			16	316	4	10	4		
8	178	3	7	4			17	191	3	4	5		
9	354	4	15	6			18	508	5	18	7		
OUT	3262			41			IN	3086	35		44		
							OUT	3262	36		41		
							TOTAL	6348	71		85		

(a)

Markers Signature _D.B._ (e & f)

Players Signature _Bill White_

HANDICAP _10_ (d)
NETT _75_

Competitor's Responsibilities:

1. To record the correct handicap somewhere on the score card before it is returned to the Committee.
2. To check the gross score recorded for each hole is correct.
3. To ensure that the marker has signed the card and to countersign the card himself before it is returned to the Committee.

Committee Responsibilities:

1. Issue to each competitor a score card containing the date and the competitor's name.
2. To add the scores for each hole and apply the handicap recorded on the card.

(**a**) Hole numbers may be altered if hole scores have been recorded in the wrong boxes.
(**b**) A marker need not keep a record of his own score, however it is recommended.
(**c**) There is nothing in the Rules that requires an alteration to be initialled.
(**d**) The competitor is responsible only for the correctness of the score recorded for each hole. If the competitor records a wrong total score or net score, the Committee must correct the error, without penalty to the competitor. In this instance, the Committee have added the scores for each hole and applied the handicap.
(**e**) There is no penalty if a marker signs the competitor's score card in the space provided for the competitor's signature, and the competitor then signs in the space provided for the marker's signature.
(**f**) The initialing of the score card by the competitor is sufficient for the purpose of countersignature.

In stroke play only, the *Committee* may, in such a condition, modify the penalty for a breach of this Rule as follows:
First offense — One stroke; Second offense — Two strokes. For subsequent offense — Disqualification.

6-8 DISCONTINUANCE OF PLAY; RESUMPTION OF PLAY
a When Permitted
The player shall not discontinue play unless:
(i)   the *Committee* has suspended play;
(ii) he believes there is danger from lightning;
(iii) he is seeking a decision from the *Committee* on a doubtful or disputed point (see Rules 2-5 and 34-3); or
(iv) there is some other good reason such as sudden illness.
Bad weather is not of itself a good reason for discontinuing play.
 If the player discontinues play without specific permission from the *Committee*, he shall report to the *Committee* as soon as practicable. If he does so and the *Committee* considers his reason satisfactory, the player incurs no penalty. Otherwise, **the player shall be disqualified**.
Exception in match play: Players discontinuing match play by agreement are not subject to disqualification unless by so doing the competition is delayed.
Note: Leaving the *course* does not of itself constitute discontinuance of play.

b Procedure When Play Suspended by Committee
When play is suspended by the *Committee*, if the players in a match or group are between the play of two holes, they shall not resume play until the *Committee* has ordered a resumption of play. If they are in the process of playing a hole, they may continue provided they do so without delay. If they choose to continue, they shall discontinue either before or immediately after completing the hole.

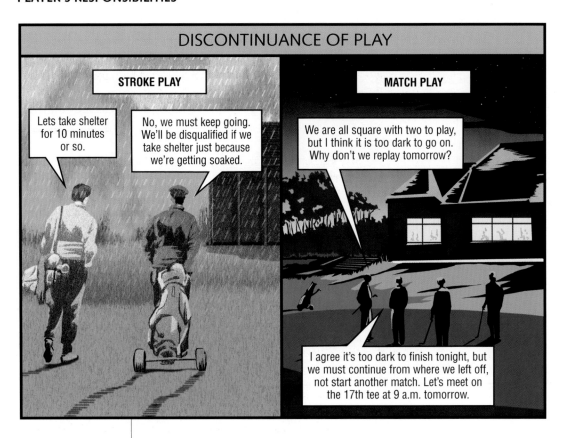

The players shall resume play when the *Committee* has ordered a resumption of play.

PENALTY FOR BREACH OF RULE 6-8b: *Disqualification*.

Note: The *Committee* may provide in the conditions of a competition (Rule 33-1) that, in potentially dangerous situations, play shall be discontinued immediately following a suspension of play by the *Committee*. If a player fails to discontinue play immediately, **he shall be disqualified** unless circumstances warrant waiving such penalty as provided in Rule 33-7.

c Lifting Ball When Play Discontinued

When a player discontinues play of a hole under Rule 6-8a, he may lift his ball without penalty only if the *Committee* has suspended play or there is a good reason to lift it. Before lifting the ball the player must mark its position. If the player discontinues play and lifts his ball without specific permission from the *Committee*, when reporting to the *Committee* (Rule 6-8a), he shall, at that time, report the lifting of the ball.

If the player lifts the ball without a good reason to do so, fails to mark the position of the ball before lifting it or fails to report the lifting of the ball, **he shall incur a penalty of one stroke**.

d Procedure When Play Resumed

Play shall be resumed from where it was discontinued, even if resumption occurs on a subsequent day. The player shall, either before or when play is resumed, proceed as follows:

(i)   if the player has lifted the ball, he shall, provided he was entitled to lift it under Rule 6-8c, place a ball on the spot from which the original ball was lifted. Otherwise, the original ball must be replaced;

(ii) if the player entitled to lift his ball under Rule 6-8c has not done so, he may lift, clean and replace the ball, or substitute a ball on the spot from which the original ball was lifted. Before lifting the ball he must mark its position; or

(iii) if the player's ball or ball-marker is moved (including by wind or water) while play is discontinued, a ball or ball-marker shall be placed on the spot from which the original ball or ball-marker was moved.

(Spot not determinable — see Rule 20-3c.)

*PENALTY FOR BREACH OF RULE 6-8d: *Match play — Loss of hole; Stroke play — Two strokes.*

   *If a player incurs the general penalty for a breach of Rule 6–8d, no additional penalty under Rule 6-8c shall be applied.

RULE 6 INCIDENTS

As the ultimate testament to a player's performance on the course in a stroke play competition, the score card must never reflect a score lower than actually taken, must be signed by the competitor, attested by the marker and returned as soon as possible to the Committee. Failure to meet any of these criteria results in disqualification.

In the excitement of Jackie Pung's apparent victory at the 1957 U.S. Women's Open Championship, the Hawaiian signed for a correct final round total of 72 but included an incorrect hole score. At the 4th hole of Winged Foot's East Course, Pung's marker had recorded a five rather than the actual score of six. A past U.S. Women's Amateur Champion and gallery favorite, Pung was told of her infraction during the post-tournament celebration. Ironically, the victory fell to Betsy Rawls, who won the 1953 Women's Open in a playoff with Pung. It was the third of Rawls' four U.S. Women's Open victories.

Roberto De Vicenzo signed for a higher score than he actually made at the 1968 Masters Tournament, which did not disqualify him but did keep the Argentinean from forcing a playoff with Bob Goalby.

Playing in front of Goalby on Sunday, De Vicenzo, the reigning British Open Champion, sank a five-foot birdie putt on the 17th hole for a 3. A bogey at the 18th gave him an 11-under total of 277. Goalby managed a five-footer for par at the 18th for a 66 and another 277.

However, De Vicenzo's fellow-competitor and marker, Tommy Aaron, had mistakenly given De Vicenzo a 4 at the 17th rather than the 3. De Vicenzo had not noticed the mistake, signed and returned the score card, and rushed away from the scorer's table for press interviews. A little later, Aaron noticed the mistake and brought it to the attention of tournament officials.

Augusta National founder Bob Jones searched for a way around the ensuing ruling but none could be found. Once the score card was signed and returned, the decision under the Rules was straightforward: the higher score must stand. Goalby was the Masters Champion.

An hour later, De Vicenzo told the media, "It's my fault. Tommy feels like I feel, very bad. I think the Rule is hard." The day's drama was compounded by the fact that it was De Vincenzo's 45th birthday.

Failure to sign a first round score card cost Padraig Harrington the 2000 Benson and Hedges International Open at The Belfry. As he began warming up for the final round, holding a five-shot lead, the 28-year-old Irishman was informed by PGA European Tour officials that he was disqualified.

Members of the Committee began collecting Harrington's three previous score cards for souvenir purposes when it was noticed that he had not signed his first round card. Jamie Spence, his marker, had signed the card as required, but Michael Campbell, the other player in the group had signed somehow instead of Harrington. The resulting penalty under Rule 6-6b was disqualification.

RULE 7

PRACTICE

DEFINITION

The *"course"* is the whole area within which play is permitted (see Rule 33-2).

7-1 BEFORE OR BETWEEN ROUNDS
a Match Play
On any day of a match play competition, a player may practice on the competition *course* before a round.

b Stroke Play
On any day of a stroke competition or play-off, a *competitor* shall not practice on the competition *course* or test the surface of any *putting green* on the *course* before a round or play-off. When two or more rounds of a stroke competition are to be played over consecutive days, a competitor shall not practice between those rounds on any competition *course* remaining to be played, or test the surface of any *putting green* on such course.
Exception: Practice putting or chipping on or near the first *teeing ground* before starting a round or play-off is permitted.
PENALTY FOR BREACH OF RULE 7-1b: *Disqualification.*
Note: The *Committee* may in the conditions of a competition (Rule 33-1) prohibit practice on the competition *course* on any day of a match play competition or permit practice on the competition *course* or part of the course (Rule 33-2c) on any day of or between rounds of a stroke competition.

7-2 DURING ROUND
A player shall not play a practice *stroke* either during the play of a hole or between the play of two holes except that, between the play of two holes, the player may practice putting or chipping on or near the *putting green* of

See **incident** involving Rule 7-2 on page 121

PRACTICE DURING A ROUND

Practice putting and chipping on or near the tee of the next hole to be played is permitted as long as play is not delayed.

See **incident** involving Rule 7-2 below

the hole last played, any practice *putting green* or the *teeing ground* of the next hole to be played in the round, provided such practice *stroke* is not played from a *hazard* and does not unduly delay play (Rule 6-7).

Strokes played in continuing the play of a hole, the result of which has been decided, are not practice *strokes*.

Exception: When play has been suspended by the *Committee*, a player may, prior to resumption of play, practise (a) as provided in this Rule, (b) anywhere other than on the competition *course* and (c) as otherwise permitted by the *Committee*.

PENALTY FOR BREACH OF RULE 7-2: *Match play — Loss of hole; Stroke play — Two strokes.*

In the event of a breach between the play of two holes, the penalty applies to the next hole.

Note 1: A practice swing is not a practice *stroke* and may be taken at any place, provided the player does not breach the *Rules*.

Note 2: The *Committee* may prohibit practice on or near the *putting green* of the hole last played.

RULE 7 INCIDENT

Vickie Odegard was penalized two strokes at the 2000 U.S. Women's Open when she dropped several balls on the back tee at the 5th hole and practiced her putting.

Under Rule 7-2, as long as it does not cause a delay, practice putting and chipping is permitted on the putting green of the last hole played or the teeing ground of the next hole to be played.

The problem was that Odegard practiced on a back tee — an area mowed as a tee — and that area was approximately 30 yards from the 5th hole's teeing ground. By definition, the teeing ground is a rectangular area two club-lengths in depth, the front and sides of which are defined by the outside limits of the two tee-markers. On the back tee, Odegard was not considered on or near the next teeing ground.

Because the infraction took place between holes, the two-stroke penalty was applied to the next hole, the 5th hole.

At the 1993 U.S. Open at Baltusrol Golf Club, during a period of slow play, Tom Watson took advantage of this Rule to practice his putting and change the momentum of his game that day. Watson's group finished play of the 5th hole and then found it necessary to wait before playing from the 6th tee. Concurrently, the group behind Watson's group had dropped far enough back so they were not in a position to play to the 5th green.

Cognizant of Rule 7-2, Watson confirmed that it was permissible for him to hit some practice putts as long as he wasn't delaying play. He then dropped a couple of balls on the green and holed some rather long putts. The confidence gained from this practice was apparently valuable because over the ensuing holes, Watson made more than one sizeable putt for birdie.

Also under Rule 7-2, the Committee may permit practice on the course after play has been suspended and prior to resumption. Thick fog forced a suspension of play during the first round of the 2000 U.S. Open at Pebble Beach. Because it was not a dangerous situation and because the Committee sanctioned it, those players who were between holes were permitted to practice under the stipulations of Rule 7-2.

When it was evident that the fog would not clear quickly, the players were evacuated from the course and returned to the clubhouse. When the first round resumed the following morning, Rule 7-2 was also applicable before the siren announced the resumption of play.

RULE ADVICE; INDICATING LINE OF PLAY

DEFINITIONS

"*Advice*" is any counsel or suggestion which could influence a player in determining his play, the choice of a club or the method of making a *stroke*.

Information on the *Rules* or on matters of public information, such as the position of *hazards* or the *flagstick* on the *putting green*, is not *advice*.

The "*line of play*" is the direction which the player wishes his ball to take after a *stroke*, plus a reasonable distance on either side of the intended direction. The *line of play* extends vertically upwards from the ground, but does not extend beyond the *hole*.

8-1 ADVICE

During a *stipulated round*, a player shall not give *advice* to anyone in the competition except his *partner* and may ask for *advice* only from his *partner* or either of their *caddies*.

See **incident** involving Rule 8-1 on page 40

8-2 INDICATING LINE OF PLAY
a Other Than on Putting Green

Except on the *putting green*, a player may have the *line of play* indicated to him by anyone, but no one shall be positioned by the player on or close to the line or an extension of the line beyond the *hole* while the *stroke* is being played. Any mark placed during the play of a hole by the player or with his knowledge to indicate the line shall be removed before the *stroke* is played.

Exception: *Flagstick* attended or held up — see Rule 17-1.

See **incident** involving Rule 8-2b below

b On the Putting Green

When the player's ball is on the *putting green*, the player, his *partner* or either of their *caddies* may, before but not during the *stroke*, point out a line for putting, but in so doing the *putting green* shall not be touched. No mark shall be placed anywhere to indicate a line for putting.

PENALTY FOR BREACH OF RULE: *Match play — Loss of hole; Stroke play — Two strokes.*

Note: The *Committee* may, in the conditions of a team competition (Rule 33-1), permit each team to appoint one person who may give *advice* (including pointing out a line for putting) to members of that team. The *Committee* may lay down conditions relating to the appointment and permitted conduct of such person, who must be identified to the *Committee* before giving *advice*.

RULE 8 INCIDENTS

During the third round of the 1991 PGA Championship while advising John Daly about the break of a putt on Crooked Stick's 11th green, Daly's caddie, Jeff "Squeeky" Medlen, accidentally touched the green with the flagstick.

As ninth alternate, Daly had been included in the championship field when Nick Price withdrew to be present for the birth of his child, and three alternates ahead of Daly declined for various reasons. The unknown Arkansan had taken the outright lead for the title after posting a 69 and 67 for the first and second rounds respectively. Playing with Bruce Lietzke on Saturday, Daly was on his way to a third round 69. At the 11th, Medlen used his hand to point out the line of Daly's first putt. In his other hand, Medlen held the flagstick and inadvertently allowed it to touch the green.

The potential infraction was televised to millions and, fortunately, videotaped for review. Alerted almost immediately to what had taken place, PGA of America Rules officials met Daly at the end of the round to discuss the matter and make a decision about a possible infraction before Daly returned his score card.

Daly, Medlen, Lietzke and Rules officials climbed into courtesy cars and rode to a television trailer to view the videotape. The tape showed Medlen holding the removed flagstick and allowing it to touch the putting green about three feet to the right of the hole while indicating the line of putt with his other hand. Rule 8-2 states that, while a line for putting may be pointed out, the green shall not be touched in doing so.

After speaking with all involved and watching the tape, the referee was convinced that Daly's left-to-right breaking putt was never in danger of reaching the spot where the flagstick had touched the green and that no mark had been left to aid Daly with the putt. Daly missed that putt, and the resulting tap-in was also unaffected by the flagstick having touched the green. No penalty was incurred. Daly returned his third round card with a score of 69. The following day, he won the PGA Championship by three shots.

On the 17th hole at Long Cove Club during the stroke play qualifying rounds of the 1991 U.S. Mid-Amateur Championship, David Eger offered his fellow-competitor a suggestion with regard to the Rules. The well-intended remark was nevertheless rewarded with a two-stroke penalty.

Previous to the remark, Eger had played his tee shot onto the putting green. The second player's tee shot had erred so far into the scrub and trees on the left that he played a provisional ball, which finished on the putting green.

As the second player went into the scrub to search for his first ball, Eger suggested it might be wiser to leave the first ball unfound and play the second ball that was already on the green in three strokes.

Information on the Rules is not advice. However, Decision 8-1/16 states that a suggestion that could influence another player "in determining his play" is advice. A Rules official overheard Eger's comment and a penalty of two strokes was assessed.

 RULE 9

INFORMATION AS TO STROKES TAKEN

9-1 GENERAL

The number of *strokes* a player has taken shall include any *penalty strokes* incurred.

9-2 MATCH PLAY

A player who has incurred a penalty shall inform his opponent as soon as practicable, unless he is obviously proceeding under a *Rule* involving a

INFORMATION AS TO STROKES TAKEN

penalty and this has been observed by his opponent. If he fails so to inform his opponent, he shall be deemed to have given wrong information, even if he was not aware that he had incurred a penalty.

An opponent is entitled to ascertain from the player, during the play of a hole, the number of *strokes* he has taken and, after play of a hole, the number of *strokes* taken on the hole just completed.

See **incident** involving Rule 9-2 below

If during the play of a hole the player gives or is deemed to give wrong information as to the number of *strokes* taken, he shall incur no penalty if he corrects the mistake before his opponent has played his next *stroke*. If the player fails so to correct the wrong information, **he shall lose the hole**.

If after play of a hole the player gives or is deemed to give wrong information as to the number of *strokes* taken on the hole just completed and this affects the opponent's understanding of the result of the hole, he shall incur no penalty if he corrects his mistake before any player plays from the next *teeing ground* or, in the case of the last hole of the match, before all players leave the *putting green*. If the player fails so to correct the wrong information, **he shall lose the hole**.

9-3 STROKE PLAY

A *competitor* who has incurred a penalty should inform his *marker* as soon as practicable.

RULE 9 INCIDENT

On the 7th tee of Kiawah Island's Ocean Course during the first morning's foursomes of the 1991 Ryder Cup Matches, Chip Beck and Paul Azinger were overheard by their European opponents discussing which type of ball they would use to optimize their performance during the play of that hole.

The Americans mistakenly believed that because one of them played a 90-compression ball and the other a 100-compression ball, they were entitled to a choice as to which they could use.

A version of the so-called one-ball Rule from the Rules of Golf's Appendix I was in effect and stipulated that a player must use the same brand and type of ball for the entire round. Whichever player's turn it was to drive was required to use the type of ball with which that player had begun the round. An option was not created just because his partner was using a different type of ball. With one player driving the odd-numbered holes and the other driving the even-numbered holes, as required during foursome competition, the Americans were mistaken in thinking they had a choice of ball types.

Unknowingly and mistakenly, the Americans made the choice and the wrong type of ball was played from the tee. The European side of Seve Ballesteros and Jose Maria Olazabal suspected this was a breach of the Rules. Sam Torrance, a European team member who was not playing in the first morning's matches, was in the gallery and following the match. He was motioned over by Ballesteros, told of the situation and sent to fetch the European Captain Bernard Gallacher.

While Gallacher was being located, play of the 7th, 8th and 9th holes was completed. On the way to the 10th tee, the Europeans made a claim concerning what had taken place at the 7th hole. The chief referee was called to settle the dispute.

In match play, Rule 9-2 requires a player who has incurred a penalty to notify his opponent as soon as practicable. If he does not, even when he doesn't know he has incurred a penalty, he is considered to have given wrong information. In this case, the American side gave wrong information as a penalty was associated with their playing of the wrong type of ball from the 7th tee. However, since the European side was aware of the error and did not make a claim (Rule 2-5) before anyone played from the 8th tee, their belated claim could not be considered. It was as if the statute of limitations had run out for that particular violation.

The match continued from the 10th tee without Beck and Azinger being penalized for their infraction at the 7th hole.

RULE **10**

ORDER OF PLAY

DEFINITION

The player who is to play first from the *teeing ground* is said to have the *"honor."*

10-1 MATCH PLAY
a Teeing Ground

The *side* which shall have the *honor* at the first *teeing ground* shall be determined by the order of the draw. In the absence of a draw, the *honor* should be decided by lot.

The *side* which wins a hole shall take the *honor* at the next *teeing ground*. If a hole has been halved, the *side* which had the *honor* at the previous *teeing ground* shall retain it.

b Other Than on Teeing Ground

When the *balls are in play*, the ball farther from the *hole* shall be played first. If the balls are equidistant from the *hole*, the ball to be played first should be decided by lot.
Exception: Rule 30-3c (best-ball and four-ball match play).

c Playing Out of Turn

If a player plays when his opponent should have played, the opponent may immediately require the player to cancel the *stroke* so played and, in correct order, play a ball without penalty as nearly as possible at the spot from which the original ball was last played (see Rule 20-5).

10-2 STROKE PLAY
a Teeing Ground

The *competitor* who shall have the *honor* at the first *teeing ground* shall be determined by the order of the draw. In the absence of a draw, the *honor* should be decided by lot.

The *competitor* with the lowest score at a *hole* shall take the *honor* at the next *teeing ground*. The *competitor* with the second lowest score shall play next and so on. If two or more *competitors* have the same score at a hole, they shall play from the next *teeing ground* in the same order as at the previous *teeing ground*.

See **incident** involving Rule 10-2b below

b Other Than on Teeing Ground

When the *balls are in play*, the ball farthest from the *hole* shall be played first. If two or more balls are equidistant from the *hole*, the ball to be played first should be decided by lot.
Exceptions: Rules 22 (ball interfering with or assisting play) and 31-5 (four-ball stroke play).

c Playing Out of Turn

If a *competitor* plays out of turn, no penalty is incurred and the ball shall be played as it lies. If, however, the *Committee* determines that *competitors* have agreed to play in an order other than that set forth in Clauses 2a, 2b and 3 of this Rule to give one of them an advantage, **they shall be disqualified.**
(Incorrect order of play in threesomes and foursomes stroke play — see Rule 29-3.)
(Playing stroke while another ball in motion after stroke from putting green — see Rule 16-1f.)

10-3 PROVISIONAL BALL OR SECOND BALL FROM TEEING GROUND

If a player plays a *provisional ball* or a second ball from a *teeing ground*, he shall do so after his opponent or *fellow-competitor* has played his first *stroke*. If a player plays a *provisional ball* or a second ball out of turn, Clauses 1c and 2c of this Rule shall apply.

10-4 BALL MOVED IN MEASURING

If a ball is *moved* in measuring to determine which ball is farther from the *hole*, no penalty is incurred and the ball shall be replaced.

RULE 10 INCIDENT

In a playoff with Lew Worsham for the 1947 U.S. Open Championship at St. Louis Country Club, Sam Snead's destiny arrived with him at the final green and the Rules played a supporting role.

Of the 1,356 entries for the championship that year it had come down to Worsham and Snead who had played the regulation 72 holes in 282 strokes — two-under-par. An eighteen-hole playoff ensued. Coming to the last hole of the playoff, Snead and Worsham were tied. After playing to the green, both men were left with putts for par from about the same distance.

Rule 10 is unequivocal regarding the order of play. In stroke play competition "When the balls are in play, the ball farthest from the hole shall be played first." It also states that in stroke play no penalty is incurred if a competitor plays out of turn, as long as it has not been agreed upon in order to give one of them an advantage.

Both balls were less than three feet from the hole. Worsham voiced no objection when Snead began his procedure for putting first. This fact would indicate that it must have been apparent to both men that Snead was away.

Snead recalls not only addressing his putt but actually taking the club back. "In the middle of my backswing, Lew said, 'Sam, I think I'm away.'" Snead interrupted his stroke.

Isaac B. Grainger of Montclair, NJ, was the Rules official with the group. "When Ike came over," Snead remembers, "I said 'I know I can continue putting and, besides, I am away as well.'"

Grainger was an authority on the Rules and would serve as president of the USGA in 1954 and 1955. He was renowned for being fastidious.

"Ike never replied," Snead recalls, "but he did have a Ruler."

The players backed slightly away and watched intently as Grainger measured from the flagstick to each ball. Snead remembers that his ball measured 30½ inches from the flagstick. The distance to Worsham's ball was 30 inches. It was, indeed, Snead's turn to play.

The interruption proved distracting. In the film, Snead appears to have lost his focus. The what-if-I-miss-it question took stage before he could simply bang the ball into the hole. Snead inexplicably missed. Worsham holed his ball for a score of 69 and the 1947 U.S. Open Championship.

RULE 11 TEEING GROUND

DEFINITION

The *"teeing ground"* is the starting place for the hole to be played. It is a rectangular area two club-lengths in depth, the front and the sides of which are defined by the outside limits of two tee-markers. A ball is outside the *teeing ground* when all of it lies outside the *teeing ground*.

11-1 TEEING

In teeing, the ball may be placed on the ground, on an irregularity of surface created by the player on the ground or on a tee, sand or other substance in order to raise it off the ground.

A player may stand outside the *teeing ground* to play a ball within it.

11-2 TEE-MARKERS

Before a player plays his first *stroke* with any ball from the *teeing ground* of the hole being played, the tee-markers are deemed to be fixed. In such circumstances, if the player moves or allows to be moved a tee-marker for the purpose of avoiding interference with his *stance*, the area of his intended swing or his *line of play*, **he shall incur the penalty for a breach of Rule 13-2.**

45

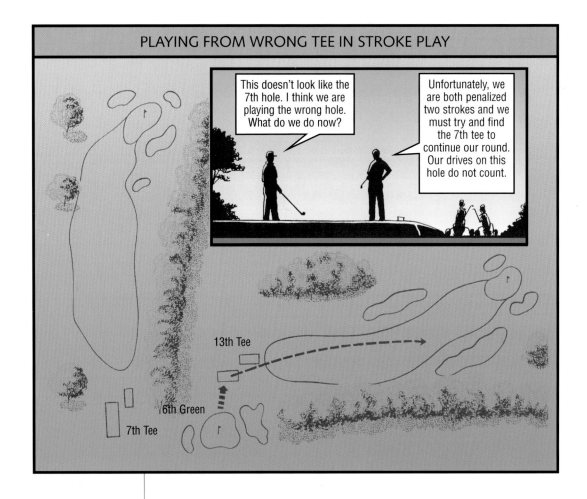

11-3 BALL FALLING OFF TEE

If a ball, when not in play, falls off a tee or is knocked off a tee by the player in *addressing* it, it may be re-teed without penalty, but if a *stroke* is made at the ball in these circumstances, whether the ball is moving or not, the *stroke* counts but no penalty is incurred.

11-4 PLAYING FROM OUTSIDE TEEING GROUND
a Match Play

If a player, when starting a hole, plays a ball from outside the *teeing ground*, the opponent may immediately require the player to cancel the *stroke* so played and play a ball from within the *teeing ground*, without penalty.

b Stroke Play

See **incident** involving Rule 11-4b on page 47

If a *competitor*, when starting a hole, plays a ball from outside the *teeing ground*, **he shall incur a penalty of two strokes** and shall then play a ball from within the *teeing ground*.

If the *competitor* plays a *stroke* from the next *teeing ground* without first correcting his mistake or, in the case of the last hole of the round, leaves the *putting green* without first declaring his intention to correct his mistake, **he shall be disqualified**.

The *stroke* from outside the *teeing ground* and any subsequent *strokes* by the *competitor* on the hole prior to his correction of the mistake do not count in his score.

11-5 PLAYING FROM WRONG TEEING GROUND
The provisions of Rule 11-4 apply.

RULE 11 INCIDENT

The result of the 1990 U.S. Open Championship lent further substantiation to the USGA's 18-hole playoff policy. A tie at eight-under-par, 280, joined Mike Donald and Hale Irwin after 72 holes of regulation play.

It would take another full trip around Medinah's No. 3 course and, even then, it would not be decided.

However, a momentary lapse of concentration regarding the Rules of Golf might have determined the winner had it not been for the diligence of the attending referee.

"After a long week, I was tired" said C. Grant Spaeth, former USGA president and the official accompanying the playoff. "Walking off the 17th green, I was tempted not to go down a hill to the 18th tee, which sits out on a peninsula that stretches into the lake.

"I thought I might cut over to the 18th fairway, contrary to the strictures in the book (the USGA manual that suggests walking Rules officials and referees be present at each teeing ground.) Thank God I resisted and trudged back to the tee."

The drama and competitive tension at Medinah Country Club had been intense all week. Irwin, 45, had summoned a wave of talent reflective of his 33 professional victories, which included two previous U.S. Open victories in 1974 and 1979. Indeed, he had holed a 45-foot birdie putt on the 72nd hole of regulation play to force the Monday playoff. Donald, 34, was the journeyman hopeful whose only PGA Tour victory had come the previous year in Williamsburg, VA.

After hours of athletic and psychological endurance, the players walked off the 17th green of the playoff round with Donald leading by one. As is sometimes the case in the waning moments of a long, intense contest, fatigue and lack of focus are cause for mistakes and lack of judgment. So it was on the 18th tee.

"If you look carefully at the films," Spaeth continues, "you will note that Mike Donald actually teed up in front of the markers, which I caught, whereupon he re-teed the ball. What an awful ending that could have been."

Rule 11, as it applies to stroke play, is exact. If a competitor plays from outside the teeing ground, he shall incur a penalty of two strokes and shall then play a ball from within the teeing ground. Had Donald's mistake been observed a few moments later, after he had played from ahead of the markers, the resulting two-stroke penalty would have given Irwin an almost insurmountable lead and the victory.

Spaeth's correction prevented the infraction, but Donald's bogey at the 90th hole resulted in both men scoring 74 in the playoff round. By the terms and conditions outlined in the entry form, and for the first time in its history, the U.S. Open then moved to sudden death to determine the winner.

On the first sudden death hole, the 91st hole of the championship, Irwin holed a eight-foot birdie putt to become the U.S. Open's oldest winner.

RULE **12** SEARCHING FOR AND IDENTIFYING BALL

DEFINITIONS

A *"hazard"* is any *bunker* or *water hazard*.

A *"bunker"* is a *hazard* consisting of a prepared area of ground, often a hollow, from which turf or soil has been removed and replaced with sand or the like. Grass-covered ground bordering or within a *bunker* is not part of the *bunker*. The margin of a *bunker* extends vertically downwards, but not upwards. A ball is in a *bunker* when it lies in or any part of it touches the *bunker*.

A "water hazard" is any sea, lake, pond, river, ditch, surface drainage ditch or other open water course (whether or not containing water) and anything of a similar nature.

All ground or water within the margin of a *water hazard* is part of the *water hazard*. The margin of a *water hazard* extends vertically upwards and downwards. Stakes and lines defining the margins of *water hazards*

SEARCHING FOR BALL IN BUNKER

If a player's ball is buried in a bunker, he may search for it by probing the sand with his fingers or he may use a rake. If the ball is moved, there is no penalty, but it must be replaced and, if necessary, re-covered so that only part of it is visible.

are in the *hazards*. Such stakes are *obstructions*. A ball is in a *water hazard* when it lies in or any part of it touches the *water hazard*.

Note 1: *Water hazards* (other than *lateral water hazards*) should be defined by yellow stakes or lines.

Note 2: The *Committee* may make a Local Rule prohibiting play from an environmentally-sensitive area which has been defined as a *water hazard*.

12-1 SEARCHING FOR BALL; SEEING BALL

See **incident** involving Rule 12-1 on page 51

In searching for his ball anywhere on the *course*, the player may touch or bend long grass, rushes, bushes, whins, heather or the like, but only to the extent necessary to find and identify it, provided that this does not improve the lie of the ball, the area of his intended swing or his *line of play*.

A player is not necessarily entitled to see his ball when playing a *stroke*.

In a *hazard*, if a ball is believed to be covered by *loose impediments* or sand, the player may remove by probing, raking or other means as much thereof as will enable him to see a part of the ball. If an excess is removed, no penalty is incurred and the ball shall be re-covered so that only a part of the ball is visible. If the ball is *moved* in such removal, no penalty is incurred; the ball shall be replaced and, if necessary, re-covered. As to removal of *loose impediments* outside a *hazard*, see Rule 23.

If a ball lying in an *abnormal ground condition* is accidentally *moved* during search, no penalty is incurred; the ball shall be replaced, unless the player elects to proceed under Rule 25-1b. If the player replaces the ball, he may still proceed under Rule 25-1b if applicable.

If a ball is believed to be lying in water in a *water hazard*, the player may probe for it with a club or otherwise. If the ball is *moved* in so doing, no penalty is incurred; the ball shall be replaced, unless the player elects to proceed under Rule 26-1.

PENALTY FOR BREACH OF RULE 12-1: *Match play — Loss of hole; Stroke play — Two strokes.*

12-2 IDENTIFYING BALL

The responsibility for playing the proper ball rests with the player. Each player should put an identification mark on his ball.

Except in a *hazard*, the player may, without penalty, lift a ball he believes to be his own for the purpose of identification and clean it to the extent necessary for identification. If the ball is the player's ball, he shall replace it. Before lifting the ball, the player must announce his intention to his opponent in match play or his *marker* or a *fellow-competitor* in stroke play and mark the position of the ball. He must then give his opponent, *marker* or *fellow-competitor* an opportunity to observe the lifting and replacement. If he lifts his ball without announcing his intention in advance, marking the position of the ball or giving his opponent, *marker* or *fellow-competitor* an opportunity to observe, or if he lifts his ball for identification in a *hazard*, or cleans it more than necessary for identification, **he shall incur a penalty of one stroke** and the ball shall be replaced.

If a player who is required to replace a ball fails to do so, **he shall incur the penalty** for a breach of Rule 20-3a, but no additional penalty under Rule 12-2 shall be applied.

Golf balls can come to rest in some odd places. At the 1992 U.S. Open, Nick Faldo scaled a tree in search of his ball that had apparently come to rest there. See the story on the next page.

RULE 12 INCIDENT

Nick Faldo discovered the Rules' protective nuances while searching for his ball in a tree at Pebble Beach's 14th hole during the 1992 U.S. Open.

His second shot at the 565-yard par 5 finished dangerously close to the right side out of bounds. For his third shot, the Englishman selected a short iron in order to play over the singular tree, which protects the elbow of the hole's second dogleg. As the ball climbed it struck the tree, but no one saw it fall back to earth.

Faldo asked the Rules official walking with the group if a provisional ball could be played. Because the official had not seen the ball come down, he replied that Faldo was entitled to play a provisional ball as the original might well be lost.

After playing the provisional ball and as they walked toward the tree to look for the original ball, the two-time British Open and two-time Masters champion asked the Rules official if it was permissible to climb the tree in order to search for his ball. The official affirmed that it was permissible, but cautioned him that if the ball moved while Faldo looked for it he would incur a penalty stroke and the ball would have to be replaced. Decision 18-2a/26 states exactly that.

However, the Rules official further advised Faldo that, if he stated his intention to declare his ball unplayable should he find it but before climbing or shaking the tree, there would be no penalty for moving the ball during the search. With such a prior notification, one penalty stroke would be assessed for a ball unplayable but no additional penalty would be incurred for moving the ball. Decision 18-2a/27 states exactly that.

Faldo listened to the advice, declared that should he find his ball he intended to proceed under the unplayable ball Rule, and then climbed the tree to search for it. Having no luck, he shook the tree in hopes of dislodging the ball. It did not appear. "Where's Jane?" he quipped while standing on a high limb.

Unable to find his original ball, Faldo's provisional ball became the ball in play under penalty of stroke and distance.

RULE  | # BALL PLAYED AS IT LIES

DEFINITIONS

A *"hazard"* is any bunker or water hazard.

A *"bunker"* is a *hazard* consisting of a prepared area of ground, often a hollow, from which turf or soil has been removed and replaced with sand or the like. Grass-covered ground bordering or within a *bunker* is not part of the *bunker*. The margin of a *bunker* extends vertically downwards, but not upwards. A ball is in a *bunker* when it lies in or any part of it touches the *bunker*.

A *"water hazard"* is any sea, lake, pond, river, ditch, surface drainage ditch or other open water course (whether or not containing water) and anything of a similar nature.

All ground or water within the margin of a *water hazard* is part of the *water hazard*. The margin of a *water hazard* extends vertically upwards and downwards. Stakes and lines defining the margins of *water hazards* are in the *hazards*. Such stakes are *obstructions*. A ball is in a *water hazard* when it lies in or any part of it touches the *water hazard*.

Note 1: *Water hazards* (other than *lateral water hazards*) should be defined by yellow stakes or lines.

Note 2: The *Committee* may make a Local Rule prohibiting play from an environmentally-sensitive area which has been defined as a *water hazard*.

The *"line of play"* is the direction which the player wishes his ball to take after a stroke, plus a reasonable distance on either side of the intended direction. The *line of play* extends vertically upwards from the ground, but does not extend beyond the *hole*.

Taking the *"stance"* consists in a player placing his feet in position for and preparatory to making a *stroke*.

13-1 GENERAL

The ball shall be played as it lies, except as otherwise provided in the *Rules*. (Ball at rest *moved* — see Rule 18).

13-2 IMPROVING LIE, AREA OF INTENDED STANCE OR SWING, OR LINE OF PLAY

See **incident** involving Rule 13-2 on page 55

Except as provided in the *Rules*, a player shall not improve or allow to be improved:

the position or lie of his ball,

the area of his intended *stance* or swing,

his *line of play* or a reasonable extension of that line beyond the *hole*, or

the area in which he is to drop or place a ball

IMPROVING AREA OF INTENDED SWING OR LINE OF PLAY

A player must not break an interfering branch or remove sand which is off the putting green but on the line of play.

CREATING OR ELIMINATING IRREGULARITIES OF SURFACE

IMPROVING AREA OF INTENDED STANCE

by any of the following actions:
moving, bending or breaking anything growing or fixed (including immovable *obstructions* and objects defining *out of bounds*), creating or eliminating irregularities of surface,
removing or pressing down sand, loose soil, replaced divots or other cut turf placed in position, or
removing dew, frost or water

53

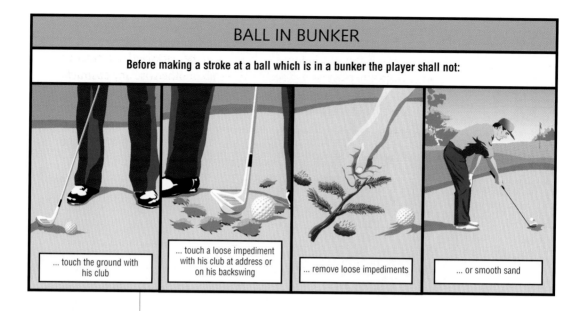

BALL IN BUNKER

Before making a stroke at a ball which is in a bunker the player shall not:

| ... touch the ground with his club | ... touch a loose impediment with his club at address or on his backswing | ... remove loose impediments | ... or smooth sand |

except as follows:

    as may occur in fairly taking his *stance*,

    in making a *stroke* or the backward movement of his club for a *stroke*,

    on the *teeing ground* in creating or eliminating irregularities of surface, or

    on the *putting green* in removing sand and loose soil as provided in Rule 16-1a or in repairing damage as provided in Rule 16-1c.

The club may be grounded only lightly and shall not be pressed on the ground.

Exception: Ball in *hazard* — see Rule 13-4.

13-3 BUILDING STANCE

A player is entitled to place his feet firmly in taking his *stance*, but he shall not build a *stance*.

13-4 BALL IN HAZARD

See **incident** involving Rule 13-4 on page 55

Except as provided in the *Rules*, before making a *stroke* at a ball which is in a *hazard* (whether a *bunker* or a *water hazard*) or which, having been lifted from a *hazard*, may be dropped or placed in the *hazard*, the player shall not:

a. Test the condition of the *hazard* or any similar *hazard*,

b. Touch the ground in the *hazard* or water in the *water hazard* with a club or otherwise, or

c. Touch or move a loose *impediment* lying in or touching the *hazard*.

Exceptions:

1. Provided nothing is done which constitutes testing the condition of the *hazard* or improves the lie of the ball, there is no penalty if the player (a) touches the ground in any *hazard* or water in a *water hazard* as a result of or to prevent falling, in removing an *obstruction*, in measuring or in retrieving, lifting, placing or replacing a ball under any *Rule* or (b) places his clubs in a *hazard*.

2. The player after playing the *stroke*, or his *caddie* at any time without the authority of the player, may smooth sand or soil in the *hazard*, provided that, if the ball is still in the *hazard*, nothing is done which improves the lie of the ball or assists the player in his subsequent play of the hole.

Note: At any time, including at *address* or in the backward movement for the *stroke*, the player may touch with a club or otherwise any *obstruction*, any construction declared by the *Committee* to be an integral part of the *course* or any grass, bush, tree or other growing thing.

PENALTY FOR BREACH OF RULE: *Match play — Loss of hole; Stroke play — Two strokes.*

(Searching for ball — see Rule 12-1.)

RULE 13 INCIDENTS

At the 2000 WGC-Andersen Consulting Match Play Championship, Tiger Woods called an infraction of Rule 13 on himself, which resulted in a loss of hole penalty. Playing La Costa Resort's 12th hole, Woods had a lie requiring him to play from under an evergreen tree.

On his backswing, Woods' club dislodged a pine cone, which fell to the ground. Woods discontinued his swing. Because he discontinued his swing and the area of his intended swing was improved, he incurred a loss of hole penalty. Had he continued his swing, there would have been no penalty as stipulated in Rule 13-2.

During the second round of the 100th U.S. Open at Pebble Beach, Bob May, in frustration, did what he innately knew he must not. May's drive at the 18th had found a horrible lie in the rough to the right of the two lone pines that guard the landing area. He took a more acute angle than needed with his second shot and the ball ran through the fairway and about four steps into the long, seaside bunker.

Left with a short iron approach, May tried for the green but advanced the ball only about 40 yards, leaving it in the bunker. Frustrated, he slapped the sand with his club.

May's fellow-competitor, Mark Brooks, approached the walking Rules official and queried, "Did you see that?" The reply was affirmative and the official walked to where May was standing.

Before anything else was said, May asked the official, "How many is that?" The reply was, "Two." To be certain, May asked the official to verify the penalty with a senior official. The two-stroke penalty was affirmed. Instead of being 3 in the bunker, he was now 5. He played the ball onto the green in 6 and two putted for a triple bogey.

In the scorer's area, Decision 13-4/35 was offered for May to read so there would be no doubt in his mind that the proper penalty had been assessed. The decision asks simply if a stroke in a bunker fails to get the ball out and the player swings his club into the sand, but his action does not affect his new lie in the bunker, is there a breach of Rule 13-4? The answer is yes, as neither of the exceptions to the Rule permits such an action.

May's two-stroke penalty put in peril his making the 36-hole cut. Fortunately, the cut came at seven-over-par and May's six-over was good enough for him to play the weekend.

RULE **14** | STRIKING THE BALL

DEFINITION

A *"stroke"* is the forward movement of the club made with the intention of fairly striking at and moving the ball, but if a player checks his down-swing voluntarily before the clubhead reaches the ball he is deemed not to have made a *stroke*.

14-1 BALL TO BE FAIRLY STRUCK AT

The ball shall be fairly struck at with the head of the club and must not be pushed, scraped or spooned.

14-2 ASSISTANCE

In making a *stroke*, a player shall not:

a. Accept physical assistance or protection from the elements, or

b. Allow his *caddie*, his *partner* or his *partner's caddie* to position himself on or close to an extension of the *line of play* or the *line of putt* behind the ball.

PENALTY FOR BREACH OF RULE 14-1 or -2: *Match play — Loss of hole; Stroke play — Two strokes.*

14-3 ARTIFICIAL DEVICES AND UNUSUAL EQUIPMENT

A player in doubt as to whether use of an item would constitute a breach of Rule 14-3 should consult the United States Golf Association.

 A manufacturer may submit to the United States Golf Association a sample of an item which is to be manufactured for a ruling as to whether its use during a *stipulated round* would cause a player to be in breach of Rule 14-3. Such sample will become the property of the United States Golf Association for reference purposes. If a manufacturer fails to submit a

BALL TO BE FAIRLY STRUCK AT WITH CLUBHEAD

A player may strike the ball with the back or toe of the clubhead.

sample before manufacturing and/or marketing the item, the manufacturer assumes the risk of a ruling that use of the item would be contrary to the Rules of Golf.

Except as provided in the *Rules*, during a *stipulated round* the player shall not use any artificial device or unusual *equipment*:

a. Which might assist him in making a *stroke* or in his play; or

b. For the purpose of gauging or measuring distance or conditions which might affect his play; or

c. Which might assist him in gripping the club, except that:

(i)   plain gloves may be worn;

See **incident** involving Rule 14-4 on page 59

(ii) resin, powder and drying or moisturising agents may be used; and

(iii) a towel or handkerchief may be wrapped around the grip.

PENALTY FOR BREACH OF RULE 14-3: *Disqualification.*

14-4 STRIKING THE BALL MORE THAN ONCE

If a player's club strikes the ball more than once in the course of a *stroke*, the player shall count the *stroke* and **add a penalty stroke**, making two strokes in all.

14-5 PLAYING MOVING BALL

A player shall not play while his ball is moving.

Exceptions:

Ball falling off tee – Rule 11-3.

Striking the ball more than once – Rule 14-4.

Ball moving in water – Rule 14-6.

When the ball begins to *move* only after the player has begun the *stroke* or the backward movement of his club for the *stroke*, he shall incur no penalty under this Rule for playing a moving ball, but he is not exempt from any penalty incurred under the following Rules:

Ball at rest *moved* by player – Rule 18-2a.

Ball at rest moving after *address* – Rule 18-2b.

Ball at rest moving after *loose impediment* touched – Rule 18-2c.

(Ball purposely deflected or stopped by player, *partner* or *caddie* – see Rule 1-2.)

14-6 BALL MOVING IN WATER

When a ball is moving in water in a *water hazard*, the player may, without penalty, make a *stroke*, but he must not delay making his *stroke* in order to allow the wind or current to improve the position of the ball. A ball moving in water in a *water hazard* may be lifted if the player elects to invoke Rule 26.

One of golf's most infamous Rules situations involved T.C. Chen at the 1985 U.S. Open. This incident, which had a dramatic effect on the final results of the championship, is retold on the next page.

PENALTY FOR BREACH OF RULE 14-5 or -6: *Match play — Loss of hole; Stroke play — Two strokes.*

RULE 14 INCIDENT

From thick rough, short and right of Oakland Hills' 5th green during the 1985 U.S. Open, T.C. Chen encountered that unfortunate fluke in golf when one swing of the club strikes the ball more than once.

Chen's third shot had left his ball about ten feet off the right front of the green and another 10 feet to the hole. He was faced with a delicate pitch shot that needed enough clubhead speed to get the lofted club through the grass but not so much that the force imparted to the ball would cause it to run beyond the hole.

Practice swings left the necessary feeling in Chen's hands for gauging the grabbing effect of the grass. He addressed the ball and swung slowly but firmly. On the downswing, as the club approached the ball, the tall grass slowed it. Chen firmly but gently pulled the club into the ball. The ball came slowly off the decelerating clubface and rose ahead of it into the air. As the club finished its path through the grass, the resistance became less and the club was released. However, the firm pulling action still left in Chen's swing gave the club added momentum as it left the grass. In a spurt of speed, the club once again caught up with the slow-moving ball and collided with it a second time. As the ball ricocheted off the clubface, a spectator rose from his kneeling position directly behind Chen with two fingers raised, indicating that the ball had been struck twice.

As the lofted clubface was going up at the moment of second impact, the ball was pushed a little higher in the air and slightly to Chen's left. It came to rest on the apron of the putting green about 10 feet from the hole.

Rule 14-4 is clear in such a situation. "If a player's club strikes the ball more than once in the course of a stroke, the player shall count the stroke and add a penalty stroke, making two strokes in all." Prior to the infraction, Chen led the championship by four strokes with 14 holes to play. Visibly shaken, he took three more to finish the hole for an eight and his hopes of winning the U.S. Open were dashed in the process. Indeed, he tied for second with Denis Watson and Dave Barr, just one shot behind Andy North.

RULE  **WRONG BALL; SUBSTITUTED BALL**

DEFINITION   A *"wrong ball"* is any ball other than the player's:
a. *Ball in play,*
b. *Provisional ball,* or
c. Second ball played under Rule 3-3 or Rule 20-7b in stroke play.
Note: *Ball in play* includes a ball substituted for the *ball in play*, whether or not such substitution is permitted.

15-1 GENERAL

A player must hole out with the ball played from the *teeing ground* unless a *Rule* permits him to substitute another ball. If a player substitutes another ball when not so permitted, that ball is not a *wrong ball*; it becomes the *ball in play* and, if the error is not corrected as provided in Rule 20-6, **the player shall incur a penalty of loss of hole in match play or two strokes in stroke play.**
(Playing from wrong place — see Rule 20–7.)

15-2 MATCH PLAY

If a player plays a *stroke* with a *wrong ball* except in a *hazard*, **he shall lose the hole**.

If a player plays any *strokes* in a *hazard* with a *wrong ball*, there is no penalty. *Strokes* played in a *hazard* with a *wrong ball* do not count in the player's score. If the *wrong ball* belongs to another player, its owner shall place a ball on the spot from which the *wrong ball* was first played.

If the player and opponent exchange balls during the play of a hole, the first to play the *wrong ball* other than from a *hazard* shall lose the hole; when this cannot be determined, the hole shall be played out with the balls exchanged.

15-3 STROKE PLAY

See **incident** involving Rule 15-3 below

If a *competitor* plays a *stroke* or *strokes* with a *wrong ball*, **he shall incur a penalty of two strokes**, unless the only *stroke* or *strokes* played with such ball were played when it was in a *hazard*, in which case no penalty is incurred.

The *competitor* must correct his mistake by playing the correct ball. If he fails to correct his mistake before he plays a *stroke* from the next *teeing ground* or, in the case of the last hole of the round, fails to declare his intention to correct his mistake before leaving the *putting green*, **he shall be disqualified**.

Strokes played by a *competitor* with a *wrong ball* do not count in his score.

If the *wrong ball* belongs to another *competitor*, its owner shall place a ball on the spot from which the *wrong ball* was first played.
(Lie of ball to be placed or replaced altered — see Rule 20-3b.)

RULE 15 INCIDENT

At the highest levels of competitive golf, it is rare that two players play each other's balls when both lie in the fairway. Brad Faxon and Phil Mickelson did exactly that at the 1995 Buick Invitational at Torrey Pines Golf Club in La Jolla, California.

Driving at the 1st hole (the player's 10th of the round having started play on the back nine), both players' balls found the fairway. Their caddies walked ahead, lowered the respective bag at their player's ball, and made a club selection. Each then played to the putting green from an unremarkable fairway lie and walked ahead to putt.

Upon marking and lifting their balls on the green, Faxon and Mickelson were stunned to see they had each played the other's ball from the fairway. At this highest level of professional golf, for neither player nor neither caddie to notice the mix-up before playing to the green may have been partially due to the mundane nature of the situation. Had one or both of the balls been in the rough, a positive identification would more likely have been made before either or both second shots were struck. As it was, the balls were about 12 feet from each other in the fairway.

As stipulated by Rule 15, both Mickelson and Faxon had played a wrong ball. While the stroke each had made with the respective wrong ball did not count in their score, two penalty strokes were assessed to each player. Both men then placed a ball on the spot from which the wrong ball was first played (where their tee shots had come to rest) and completed the hole.

Because both players corrected their mistake before playing from the next tee, there was no danger of disqualification for this infraction. While the consequences for playing a wrong ball lies squarely with the player, it would be reasonable to assume after this infraction that a conversation about how such a mistake could have happened took place between the players and their caddies.

RULE **16** | # THE PUTTING GREEN

DEFINITIONS

The *"putting green"* is all ground of the hole being played which is specially prepared for putting or otherwise defined as such by the *Committee*. A ball is on the *putting green* when any part of it touches the *putting green*.

The *"line of putt"* is the line which the player wishes his ball to take after a *stroke* on the *putting green*. Except with respect to Rule 16-1e, the *line of putt* includes a reasonable distance on either side of the intended line. The *line of putt* does not extend beyond the *hole*.

A ball is *"holed"* when it is at rest within the circumference of the *hole* and all of it is below the level of the lip of the *hole*.

16-1 GENERAL
a Touching Line of Putt
The *line of putt* must not be touched except:
(i)   the player may move sand and loose soil on the *putting green* and other *loose impediments* by picking them up or by brush ing them aside with his hand or a club without pressing anything down;
(ii)   in *addressing the ball*, the player may place the club in front of the ball without pressing anything down;
(iii)   in measuring — Rule 10-4;
(iv)   in lifting the ball — Rule 16-1b;

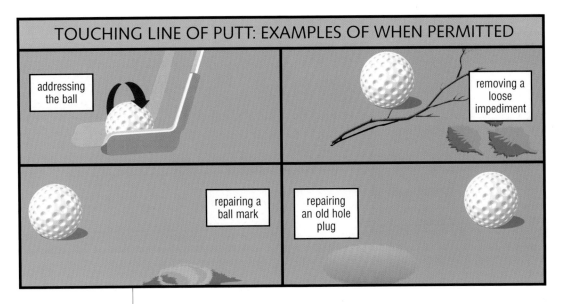

TOUCHING LINE OF PUTT: EXAMPLES OF WHEN PERMITTED

addressing the ball

removing a loose impediment

repairing a ball mark

repairing an old hole plug

(v)   in pressing down a ball-marker;

(vi)   in repairing old *hole* plugs or ball marks on the *putting green* —
       Rule 16-1c; and

(vii) in removing movable *obstructions* — Rule 24-1.

(Indicating line for putting on *putting green* — see Rule 8-2b.)

b Lifting Ball

A ball on the *putting green* may be lifted and, if desired, cleaned.
A ball so lifted shall be replaced on the spot from which it was
lifted.

See **incident**
involving Rule
16-1b on page 84

PROCEDURE FOR MARKING THE BALL

Do I have to use a ball-marker to mark my ball?

No. Although you are recommended to use a ball-marker or small coin, you may use something else like a tee or the putter head.

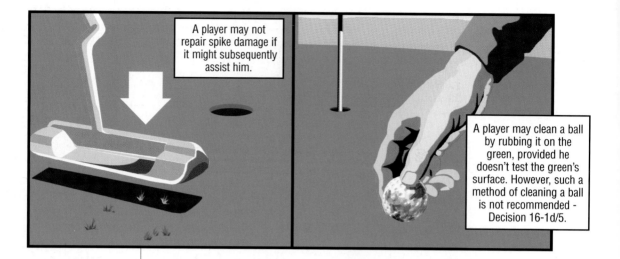

A player may not repair spike damage if it might subsequently assist him.

A player may clean a ball by rubbing it on the green, provided he doesn't test the green's surface. However, such a method of cleaning a ball is not recommended - Decision 16-1d/5.

c Repair of Hole Plugs, Ball Marks and Other Damage

The player may repair an old *hole* plug or damage to the *putting green* caused by the impact of a ball, whether or not the player's ball lies on the *putting green*. If a ball or ball-marker is accidentally *moved* in the process of such repair, the ball or ball marker shall be replaced, without penalty. Any other damage to the *putting green* shall not be repaired if it might assist the player in his subsequent play of the hole.

d Testing Surface

During the play of a hole, a player shall not test the surface of the *putting green* by rolling a ball or roughening or scraping the surface.

e Standing Astride or On Line of Putt

The player shall not make a *stroke* on the *putting green* from a *stance* astride, or with either foot touching, the *line of putt* or an extension of that line behind the ball.

f Playing Stroke While Another Ball in Motion

The player shall not play a *stroke* while another ball is in motion after a *stroke* from the *putting green*, except that, if a player does so, he incurs no penalty if it was his turn to play.

(Lifting ball interfering with or assisting play while another ball in motion — see Rule 22.)

PENALTY FOR BREACH OF RULE 16-1: *Match play* — *Loss of hole*; *Stroke play* — *Two strokes.*

(Position of *caddie* or *partner* — see Rule 14-2.)

(*Wrong putting green* — see Rule 25-3.)

16-2 BALL OVERHANGING HOLE

See **incidents** involving Rule 16-2 on page 65

When any part of the ball overhangs the lip of the *hole*, the player is allowed enough time to reach the *hole* without unreasonable delay and an additional ten seconds to determine whether the ball is at rest. If by then the ball has not fallen into the *hole*, it is deemed to be at rest. If the ball subsequently falls into the *hole*, the player is deemed to have *holed* out

with his last *stroke*, and **he shall add a *penalty stroke* to his score** for the hole; otherwise there is no penalty under this Rule.
(Undue delay — see Rule 6-7.)

RULE 16 INCIDENTS

The Rule dealing with a ball overhanging the hole was revised as a result of an incident involving Denis Watson during play of the 8th hole in the first round of the 1985 U.S. Open at Oakland Hills Country Club.

From 10 feet, Watson putted and his ball stopped on the lip of the hole. After waiting an extended period of time, the ball fell in. Subsequently, Watson was told to add two penalty strokes to his score for undue delay as described at the time in Rule 16-1h.

The severe ramification of the penalty would not be clear for three more days when Watson would finish just one stroke behind the champion, Andy North.

In 1988, the Rule was moved to Rule 16-2 and a one-stroke penalty assigned to any infraction. However, Brian Gay discovered at the 2000 Honda Classic that the application of Rule 16 is literal and the ramifications can still be severe.

On the 17th hole of the final round, Gay found himself needing a 30-foot birdie putt to draw even with Dudley Hart, who had just finished his round with a tap-in birdie at the 18th. Gay played a smooth, well-read putt, which stopped on the edge of the front lip of the hole.

Gay walked to the hole, waited 13 seconds and then watched as the ball fell in. The scoreboard recorded the birdie and Gay played the final hole believing a two-putt par would force a playoff. From 100 feet away, Gay three putted the 18th and the victory was Hart's.

As it turned out, however, Gay had not birdied the 17th because he had incurred a penalty stroke under Rule 16-2. After multiple viewings of the videotape, it was clear to the PGA Tour Rules official, Slugger White, that there was an infraction and Gay had to sign for a par 4 at the 17th rather than a 3.

"I looked at the tape 10 times," White said, "and he (Gay) and I looked at the tape another five or six times. We rolled it, we backed it up, we did everything."

The infraction was clear to the official. "It's not something you like to do," said White. "But in all honesty, he walked up to the hole. He didn't run to the hole. He did exactly what he was supposed to do."

While the three putt at the 18th had eliminated Gay's chance of winning, the penalty stroke under Rule 16-2 moved him from a tie for second to a tie for fourth.

RULE **17**

THE FLAGSTICK

DEFINITION

The *"flagstick"* is a movable straight indicator, with or without bunting or other material attached, centred in the *hole* to show its position. It shall be circular in cross-section.

See **incident** involving Rule 17-1 on page 69

17-1 FLAGSTICK ATTENDED, REMOVED OR HELD UP

Before and during the *stroke*, the player may have the *flagstick* attended, removed or held up to indicate the position of the *hole*. This may be done only on the authority of the player before he plays his *stroke*.

If, prior to the *stroke*, the *flagstick* is attended, removed or held up by anyone with the player's knowledge and no objection is made, the player shall be deemed to have authorized it. If anyone attends or holds up the *flagstick* or stands near the *hole* while a *stroke* is being played, he shall be deemed to be attending the *flagstick* until the ball comes to rest.

17-2 UNAUTHORIZED ATTENDANCE
a Match Play

In match play, an opponent or his *caddie* shall not, without the authority or prior knowledge of the player, attend, remove or hold up the *flagstick* while the player is making a *stroke* or his ball is in motion.

b Stroke Play

In stroke play, if a *fellow-competitor* or his *caddie* attends, removes or holds up the *flagstick* without the *competitor's* authority or prior knowledge while the *competitor* is making a *stroke* or his ball is in motion, **the *fellow-competitor* shall incur the penalty** for breach of this Rule. In such circumstances, if the *competitor's* ball strikes the *flagstick*, the person attending it or anything

carried by him, the *competitor* incurs no penalty and the ball shall be played as it lies, except that, if the *stroke* was played from the *putting green*, the *stroke* shall be cancelled, the ball replaced and the *stroke* replayed.

PENALTY FOR BREACH OF RULE 17-1 or -2: *Match play — Loss of hole; Stroke play — Two strokes.*

See **incident**
involving Rule 17-3
on page 69

17-3 BALL STRIKING FLAGSTICK OR ATTENDANT

The player's ball shall not strike:

a. The *flagstick* when attended, removed or held up by the player, his *partner* or either of their *caddies*, or by another person with the player's authority or prior knowledge; or

b. The player's *caddie*, his *partner* or his *partner's caddie* when attending the *flagstick*, or another person attending the *flagstick* with the player's authority or prior knowledge or anything carried by any such person; or

c. The *flagstick* in the *hole*, unattended, when the ball has been played from the *putting green*.

PENALTY FOR BREACH OF RULE 17-3: *Match play — Loss of hole; Stroke play — Two strokes, and the ball shall be played as it lies.*

The shape and contours of the 17th green at Pebble Beach Golf Links resulted in an unusual sight at the 2000 U.S. Open. For the details of this incident, involving eventual runner-up Miguel Angel Jimenez, see the story on the next page.

17-4 BALL RESTING AGAINST FLAGSTICK

If the ball rests against the *flagstick* when it is in the *hole*, the player or another person authorised by him may move or remove the *flagstick* and if the ball falls into the *hole*, the player shall be deemed to have *holed* out with his last *stroke*; otherwise the ball, if *moved*, shall be placed on the lip of the *hole*, without penalty.

RULE 17 INCIDENT

While Rule 4 stipulates the characteristics of a golf club, nowhere in the Rules is it stated where a particular club must be used. Any club can be used from anywhere on the golf course.

Golf requires imagination and some holes demand more than others. An apocryphal story is told about Pebble Beach's par-3 7th hole on a day when the wind blew so hard into the face of the players that even a three iron was not enough to reach the green 110 yards away. Having watched his fellow-competitors challenge the wind unsuccessfully, Sam Snead used a putter to run the ball down the walking path from the tee to the greenside rough at the bottom of the hill. From there, he chipped on and one-putted for par.

Miguel Angel Jimenez found himself in an awkward situation on Pebble Beach's 17th green during the 2000 U.S. Open. When H. Chandler Egan made design changes to the course prior to the 1929 U.S. Amateur Championship, one of those changes included redesigning the 17th green into a large hourglass shape divided by a diagonal ridge. The ridge running through its center makes it play like a double green. Hence, when the hole is cut at point B, it is difficult for a ball played from point A to get close to the hole. This was Jimenez's dilemma, as illustrated by the photograph on the previous page.

The pinched, hourglass shape brought the rough into the line of putt necessary for him to get close to the hole. For this reason, he chose to play a pitch shot from over the rough and over the ridge to the hole on the other side of the green.

Because it happens so infrequently and because care of the putting surface is an integral part of playing golf, it is disorienting to contemplate playing a pitch shot from the green. However, it is essential to remember that the location of the ball on the putting green, not the club used to strike it, dictates the Rules issues. A pitch shot may not be a putt, but the fact that it is being played from the putting green brings all respective Rules into play.

Jimenez was aware of the Rules regarding the flagstick, but he wisely sought confirmation from the referee walking with his group. Rule 17-3 states that a player's ball shall not strike the flagstick in the hole, unattended, when the ball has been played from the green. In order to avoid such an infraction, Jimenez directed his caddie to attend the flagstick.

Rule 17-3 also states that it is an infraction for a ball to strike an attended flagstick regardless from where the shot has been played.

Therefore, Jimenez's caddie would be required to remove the flagstick if it looked as though the ball might go in the hole.

Playing a delicate pitch, Jimenez took a small divot. His ball landed on the down slope of the ridge and ran to about 10 feet from the hole. From there he took two putts for bogey.

RULE **18** | BALL AT REST MOVED

DEFINITIONS

A ball is deemed to have *"moved"* if it leaves its position and comes to rest in any other place.

An *"outside agency"* is any agency not part of the match or, in stroke play, not part of the *competitor's side*, and includes a *referee*, a *marker*, an *observer* and a *forecaddie*. Neither wind nor water is an *outside agency*.

"Equipment" is anything used, worn or carried by or for the player except any ball he has played at the hole being played and any small object, such as a coin or a tee, when used to mark the position of a ball or the extent of an area in which a ball is to be dropped. *Equipment* includes a golf cart, whether or not motorized. If such a cart is shared by two or more players, the cart and everything in it are deemed to be the *equipment* of the player whose ball is involved except that, when the cart is being moved by one of the players sharing it, the cart and everything in it are deemed to be that player's *equipment*.

Note: A ball played at the hole being played is *equipment* when it has been lifted and not put back into play.

A player has *"addressed the ball"* when he has taken his *stance* and has also grounded his club, except that in a *hazard* a player has *addressed the ball* when he has taken his *stance*.

Taking the *"stance"* consists in a player placing his feet in position for and preparatory to making a *stroke*.

18-1 BY OUTSIDE AGENCY

See **incident** involving Rule 18-1 on page 115

If a ball at rest is *moved* by an *outside agency*, the player shall incur no penalty and the ball shall be replaced before the player plays another *stroke*. (Player's ball at rest *moved* by another ball — see Rule 18-5.)

18-2 BY PLAYER, PARTNER, CADDIE OR EQUIPMENT
a General

See **incidents** involving Rule 18-2a on page 73

When a player's *ball is in play*, if:

(i) the player, his *partner* or either of their *caddies* lifts or *moves* it, touches it purposely (except with a club in the act of *addressing* it) or causes it to *move* except as permitted by a *Rule*, or

(ii) *equipment* of the player or his *partner* causes the ball to *move*, **the player shall incur a penalty stroke**. The ball shall be replaced unless the movement of the ball occurs after the player has begun his swing and he does not discontinue his swing.

BALL AT REST MOVED

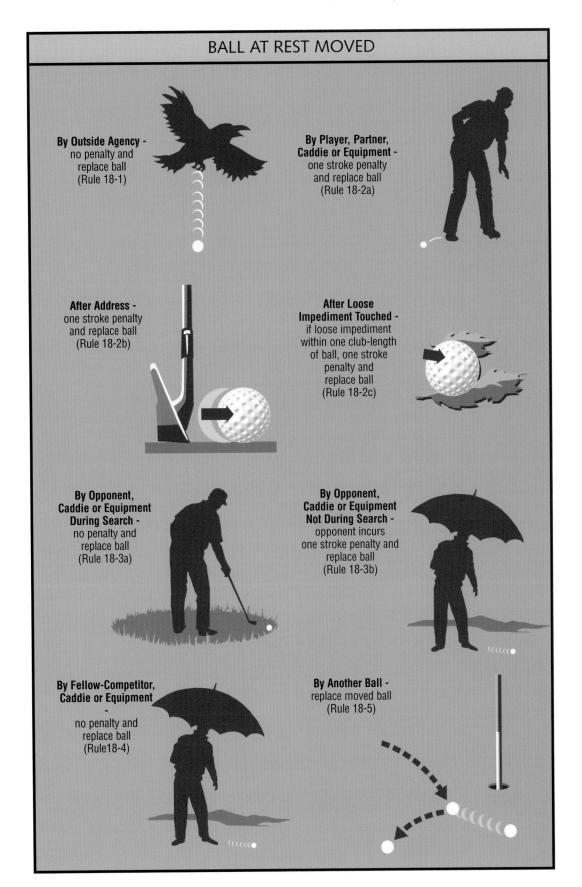

By Outside Agency - no penalty and replace ball (Rule 18-1)

By Player, Partner, Caddie or Equipment - one stroke penalty and replace ball (Rule 18-2a)

After Address - one stroke penalty and replace ball (Rule 18-2b)

After Loose Impediment Touched - if loose impediment within one club-length of ball, one stroke penalty and replace ball (Rule 18-2c)

By Opponent, Caddie or Equipment During Search - no penalty and replace ball (Rule 18-3a)

By Opponent, Caddie or Equipment Not During Search - opponent incurs one stroke penalty and replace ball (Rule 18-3b)

By Fellow-Competitor, Caddie or Equipment - no penalty and replace ball (Rule18-4)

By Another Ball - replace moved ball (Rule 18-5)

Under the *Rules* no penalty is incurred if a player accidentally causes his ball to *move* in the following circumstances:

In measuring to determine which ball farther from *hole* – Rule 10-4

In searching for covered ball in *hazard* or for ball in an *abnormal ground condition* – Rule 12-1

In the process of repairing *hole* plug or ball mark – Rule 16-1c

In the process of removing *loose impediments* on *putting green* – Rule 18-2c

In the process of lifting ball under a *Rule* – Rule 20-1.

In the process of placing or replacing ball under a *Rule* – Rule 20-3a

In removal of movable *obstruction* – Rule 24-1

b Ball Moving After Address

See **incident** involving Rule 18-2b on page 73

If a player's *ball in play moves* after he has *addressed* it (other than as a result of a *stroke*), the player shall be deemed to have *moved* the ball and **shall incur a *penalty stroke*.** The player shall replace the ball unless the movement of the ball occurs after he has begun his swing and he does not discontinue his swing.

c Ball Moving After Loose Impediment Touched

Through the green, if the ball *moves* after any *loose impediment*, lying within a club-length of it has been touched by the player, his *partner* or either of their *caddies* and before the player has *addressed* it, the player shall be deemed to have *moved* the ball and **shall incur a *penalty stroke***. The player shall replace the ball unless the movement of the ball occurs after he has begun his swing and he does not discontinue his swing.

On the *putting green*, if the ball or the ball-marker *moves* in the process of removing any *loose impediment*, the ball or the ball-marker shall be replaced. There is no penalty provided the movement of the ball or the ball-marker is directly attributable to the removal of the *loose impediment*.

Otherwise, **the player shall incur a *penalty stroke*** under Rule 18-2a or 20-1.

18-3 BY OPPONENT, CADDIE OR EQUIPMENT IN MATCH PLAY
a During Search

If, during search for a player's ball, the ball is *moved* by an opponent, his *caddie* or his *equipment*, no penalty is incurred and the player shall replace the ball.

b Other Than During Search

See **incident** involving Rule 18-3b on page 84

If, other than during search for a ball, the ball is touched or *moved* by an opponent, his *caddie* or his *equipment,* except as otherwise provided in the Rules, **the opponent shall incur a *penalty stroke***. The player shall replace the ball.

(Ball *moved* in measuring to determine which ball farther from the *hole* – see Rule 10-4.)

(Playing a *wrong ball* – see Rule 15-2.)

18-4 BY FELLOW-COMPETITOR, CADDIE OR EQUIPMENT IN STROKE PLAY

If a *competitor's* ball is *moved* by a *fellow-competitor*, his *caddie* or his *equipment*, no penalty is incurred. The *competitor* shall replace his ball.

(Playing a *wrong ball* – see Rule 15-3.)

18-5 BY ANOTHER BALL

If a *ball in play* and at rest is *moved* by another ball in motion after a *stroke*, the *moved* ball shall be replaced.

*PENALTY FOR BREACH OF RULE: *Match play — Loss of hole; Stroke play — Two strokes.*

If a player who is required to replace a ball fails to do so, he shall incur the general penalty for breach of Rule 18 but no additional penalty under Rule 18 shall be applied.

Note 1: If a ball to be replaced under this Rule is not immediately recoverable, another ball may be substituted.

Note 2: If it is impossible to determine the spot on which a ball is to be placed, see Rule 20-3c.

RULE 18 INCIDENTS

At the 1925 U.S. Open Championship at Worcester Country Club. in Massachusetts, Bobby Jones saw his ball move after he addressed it on a steep bank at the 11th hole during the first round. Jones insisted that a penalty be added to his score. Often the player may be the only one who sees such an infraction and, in such circumstances, must call the penalty on himself.

When praised for his honesty, Jones replied, "You just might as well praise me for not breaking into banks. There is only one way to play this game."

Jones began the final round in a tie for fourth place and was able to tie Willie Macfarlane to force a 36-hole playoff, which he lost 75-73 to 75-72. While leading the first round of the 1992 U.S. Women's Open at Oakmont Country Club, Donna Andrews' ball was on the apron just over the 17th putting green. Tall rough crowded the ball at the back. As she practiced the stroke for her difficult putt, Andrews' club unintentionally bumped and moved the ball about five inches. Realizing her misfortune, Andrews gathered her concentration and finished the hole from the ball's new location.

Because she had not intended to strike the ball, a "stroke" had not been made. However, two penalty strokes were levied because she caused the ball to move and did not replace it before playing again. Fortunately, the infraction was seen on television and Andrews was alerted to the penalty before signing and returning her score card thus avoiding disqualification.

Davis Love III was not so fortunate during The Players Championship in 1997. While executing his pre-shot routine before putting at the 17th, Love's putter accidentally moved his ball about an inch. Failing to replace the moved ball, he two putted and went to the 18th tee. Assessing himself one stroke for moving his ball rather than the total penalty of two strokes for moving and not replacing his ball, Love recorded a four on his score card instead of a five.

Although viewed by thousands in person, the error was not brought to Love's attention until after his scorecard had been returned. The result was disqualification.

RULE **19**

BALL IN MOTION DEFLECTED OR STOPPED

DEFINITIONS

An *"outside agency"* is any agency not part of the match or, in stroke play, not part of the *competitor's side*, and includes a *referee*, a *marker*, an *observer* and a *forecaddie*. Neither wind nor water is an *outside agency*.

"*Equipment*" is anything used, worn or carried by or for the player except any ball he has played at the hole being played and any small object, such as a coin or a tee, when used to mark the position of a ball or the extent of an area in which a ball is to be dropped. *Equipment* includes a golf cart, whether or not motorized. If such a cart is shared by two or more players, the cart and everything in it are deemed to be the *equipment* of the player whose ball is involved except that, when the cart is being moved by one of the players sharing it, the cart and everything in it are deemed to be that player's *equipment*.

Note: A ball played at the hole being played is *equipment* when it has been lifted and not put back into play.

19-1 BY OUTSIDE AGENCY

See **incident** involving Rule 19-1 on page 76

If a ball in motion is accidentally deflected or stopped by any *outside agency*, it is a *rub of the green*, no penalty is incurred and the ball shall be played as it lies except:

a. If a ball in motion after a *stroke* other than on the *putting green* comes to rest in or on any moving or animate *outside agency*, the player shall, *through the green* or in a *hazard*, drop the ball, or on the *putting green* place the ball, as near as possible to the spot where the *outside agency* was when the ball came to rest in or on it, and

b. If a ball in motion after a *stroke* on the *putting green* is deflected or stopped by, or comes to rest in or on, any moving or animate *outside agency* except a worm or an insect, the *stroke* shall be cancelled, the ball replaced and the *stroke* replayed.

If the ball is not immediately recoverable, another ball may be substituted.

(Player's ball deflected or stopped by another ball — see Rule 19-5.)

Note: If the *referee* or the *Committee* determines that a player's ball has been purposely deflected or stopped by an *outside agency*, Rule 1-4 applies to the player. If the *outside agency* is a *fellow-competitor* or his *caddie*, Rule 1-2 applies to the *fellow-competitor*.

19-2 BY PLAYER, PARTNER, CADDIE OR EQUIPMENT

a Match Play

If a player's ball is accidentally deflected or stopped by himself, his *partner* or either of their *caddies* or *equipment*, **he shall lose the hole**.

b Stroke Play

If a *competitor's* ball is accidentally deflected or stopped by himself, his *partner* or either of their *caddies* or *equipment*, **the *competitor* shall incur a penalty of two strokes**. The ball shall be played as it lies, except when it comes to rest in or on the *competitor's*, his *partner's* or either of their

BALL IN MOTION DEFLECTED OR STOPPED

By Player, Partner, Caddie or Equipment Match Play - player loses hole (Rule 19-2a)

By Player, Partner, Caddie or Equipment Stroke Play - player incurs penalty of two strokes and ball played as it lies (Rule 19-2b)

By Outside Agency - no penalty and ball played as it lies (Rule 19-1)

By Opponent, Caddie or Equipment Match Play - no penalty and ball played as it lies or stroke cancelled and replayed (Rule 19-3)

By Fellow-Competitor, Caddie or Equipment Stroke Play - see Rule 19-1 regarding ball deflected by Outside Agency (Rule 19-4)

By Another Ball at Rest - no penalty and ball played as it lies. Except in stroke play, if both balls lay on green prior to stroke, player incurs two stroke penalty (Rule 19-5a)

By Another Ball in Motion - no penalty and ball played as it lies, unless player in breach of Rule 16-1f (Rule 19-5b)

caddies' clothes or *equipment*, in which case the *competitor* shall *through the green* or in a *hazard* drop the ball, or on the *putting green* place the ball, as near as possible to where the article was when the ball came to rest in or on it.

Exception: Dropped Ball — see Rule 20-2a.

(Ball purposely deflected or stopped by player, *partner* or *caddie* — see Rule 1-2.)

19-3 BY OPPONENT, CADDIE OR EQUIPMENT IN MATCH PLAY

If a player's ball is accidentally deflected or stopped by an opponent, his *caddie* or his *equipment*, no penalty is incurred. The player may play the ball as it lies or, before another *stroke* is played by either *side*, cancel the *stroke* and play a ball without penalty as nearly as possible at the spot from which the original ball was last played (see Rule 20-5).

If the ball has come to rest in or on the opponent's or his *caddie's* clothes or *equipment*, the player may *through the green* or in a *hazard* drop the ball, or on the *putting green* place the ball, as near as possible to where the article was when the ball came to rest in or on it.

Exception: Ball striking person attending *flagstick* — see Rule 17-3b.

(Ball purposely deflected or stopped by opponent or *caddie* — see Rule 1-2.)

19-4 BY FELLOW-COMPETITOR, CADDIE OR EQUIPMENT IN STROKE PLAY

See Rule 19-1 regarding ball deflected by *outside agency*.

19-5 BY ANOTHER BALL
a At Rest

If a player's ball in motion after a *stroke* is deflected or stopped by a *ball in play* and at rest, the player shall play his ball as it lies. In match play, no penalty is incurred. In stroke play, there is no penalty unless both balls lay on the *putting green* prior to the *stroke*, in which case **the player incurs a penalty of two strokes.**

b In Motion

If a player's ball in motion after a *stroke* is deflected or stopped by another ball in motion after a *stroke*, the player shall play his ball as it lies. There is no penalty unless the player was in breach of Rule 16-1f, in which case **he shall incur the penalty for breach of that Rule.**

Exception: If the player's ball is in motion after a *stroke* on the *putting green* and the other ball in motion is an *outside agency* — see Rule 19-1b.

PENALTY FOR BREACH OF RULE: *Match play* — Loss of hole; *Stroke play* — Two strokes.

See **incident** involving Rule 19-5 below

RULE 19 INCIDENTS

During the 1989 U.S. Women's Open at Indianwood Golf and Country Club in Lake Orion, Mich., Patty Sheehan's approach to the 18th hole struck Colleen Walker's ball and moved it about six feet closer to the hole.

Sheehan had played her approach shot from an elevated position at the left of the large, bowl-shaped green. The ball had plenty of momentum as it landed and ran smoothly and squarely into Walker's ball.

Rule 18-5 requires that when a ball in play and at rest is moved by another ball in motion after a stroke, the moved ball must be replaced.

The Rules generally entitle a player to the lie that her stroke gave her. Had Walker's ball been knocked into a water hazard or bunker, she would be returned to her original lie on the putting green. Had Walker's ball been knocked into the hole, it would also be replaced at its original position.

Sheehan, on the other hand, was required by Rule 19-5 to play her ball as it lay. Had Sheehan's ball been deflected into the hole, it would have been holed. Conversely, had Sheehan's ball been deflected out of bounds, the stroke and distance penalty would have been assessed. In this case, Sheehan was left with a makeable putt for birdie.

Sergio Garcia encountered a similar situation when his drive at Pebble Beach's 4th hole struck and killed a seagull during the second round of the 2000 U.S. Open.

The bird swooped down into the ball's path just 20 yards from the teeing ground. Traveling with great velocity, the ball struck the bird in the chest. The gull was killed. Somehow, the ball continued on in a decelerated way until it struck the top of the out of bounds fence, which shelters the beach club parking lot to the right. One bounce atop the picket fence and the ball was deflected back onto the course, where it settled in the rough.

Garcia was distraught by the bird's death and the bizarre rub of the green. In such a situation, no penalty is incurred and the ball must be played as it lies. At first, many of the assembled spectators thought such a ruling was unfair and Garcia should be allowed to replay the shot. Their concern was assuaged when it was pointed out that had Garcia's ball been deflected into the hole it would have been a hole-in-one.

RULE **20**

LIFTING, DROPPING AND PLACING; PLAYING FROM WRONG PLACE

See **incident** involving Rule 20-1 on page 84

20-1 LIFTING AND MARKING

A ball to be lifted under the *Rules* may be lifted by the player, his *partner* or another person authorised by the player. In any such case, the player shall be responsible for any breach of the *Rules*.

The position of the ball shall be marked before it is lifted under a *Rule* which requires it to be replaced. If it is not marked, **the player shall incur a penalty of one stroke** and the ball shall be replaced. If it is not replaced, the player shall incur the general penalty for breach of this Rule but no additional penalty under Rule 20-1 shall be applied.

77

If a ball or ball-marker is accidentally *moved* in the process of lifting the ball under a *Rule* or marking its position, the ball or the ball-marker shall be replaced. There is no penalty provided the movement of the ball or the ball-marker is directly attributable to the specific act of marking the position of or lifting the ball. Otherwise, **the player shall incur a *penalty stroke*** under this Rule or Rule 18-2a.

Exception: If a player incurs a penalty for failing to act in accordance with Rule 5-3 or 12-2, no additional penalty under Rule 20-1 shall be applied.

Note: The position of a ball to be lifted should be marked by placing a ball-marker, a small coin or other similar object immediately behind the ball. If the ball-marker interferes with the play, *stance* or *stroke* of another player, it should be placed one or more clubhead-lengths to one side.

20-2 DROPPING AND RE-DROPPING
a By Whom and How

See **incident** involving Rule 20-2a on page 84

A ball to be dropped under the *Rules* shall be dropped by the player himself. He shall stand erect, hold the ball at shoulder height and arm's length and drop it. If a ball is dropped by any other person or in any other manner and the error is not corrected as provided in Rule 20-6, **the player shall incur a *penalty stroke***.

If the ball touches the player, his *partner*, either of their *caddies* or their *equipment* before or after it strikes a part of the *course*, the ball shall be re-dropped, without penalty. There is no limit to the number of times a ball shall be re-dropped in such circumstances.

(Taking action to influence position or movement of ball — see Rule 1-2.)

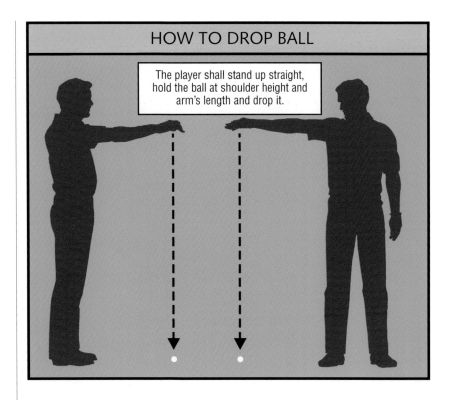

HOW TO DROP BALL

The player shall stand up straight, hold the ball at shoulder height and arm's length and drop it.

b Where to Drop

When a ball is to be dropped as near as possible to a specific spot, it shall be dropped not nearer the *hole* than the specific spot which, if it is not precisely known to the player, shall be estimated.

A ball when dropped must first strike a part of the *course* where the applicable *Rule* requires it to be dropped. If it is not so dropped, Rules 20-6 and -7 apply.

c When to Re-Drop

A dropped ball shall be re-dropped without penalty if it:

(i)   rolls into and comes to rest in a *hazard*;

(ii)   rolls out of and comes to rest outside a *hazard*;

(iii)   rolls onto and comes to rest on a *putting green*;

(iv)   rolls and comes to rest *out of bounds*;

(v)   rolls to and comes to rest in a position where there is interference by the condition from which relief was taken under Rule 24-2 (immovable *obstruction*), Rule 25-1 (*abnormal ground conditions*), Rule 25-3 (*wrong putting green*) or a Local Rule (Rule 33-8a), or rolls back into the pitch-mark from which it was lifted under Rule 25-2 (embedded ball);

(vi)   rolls and comes to rest more than two club-lengths from where it first struck a part of the *course*;

(vii) rolls and comes to rest nearer the *hole* than:

    a. its original position or estimated position (see Rule 20-2b) unless otherwise permitted by the *Rules*; or

    b. the *nearest point of relief* or maximum available relief (Rule 24-2, 25-1 or 25-3); or

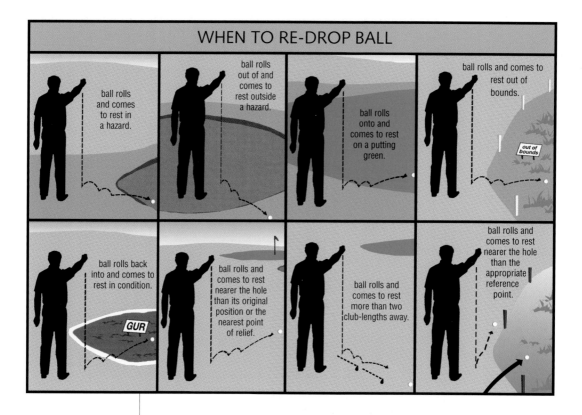

c. the point where the original ball last crossed the margin of the *water hazard* or *lateral water hazard* (Rule 26-1).

If the ball when re-dropped rolls into any position listed above, it shall be placed as near as possible to the spot where it first struck a part of the *course* when re-dropped.

If a ball to be re-dropped or placed under this Rule is not immediately recoverable, another ball may be substituted.

Note: If a ball when dropped or re-dropped comes to rest and subsequently *moves*, the ball shall be played as it lies, unless the provisions of any other *Rule* apply.

20-3 PLACING AND REPLACING
a By Whom and Where

See **incident** involving Rule 20-3a on page 84

A ball to be placed under the *Rules* shall be placed by the player or his *partner*. If a ball is to be replaced, the player, his *partner* or the person who lifted or *moved* it shall place it on the spot from which it was lifted or *moved*. In any such case, the player shall be responsible for any breach of the *Rules*.

If a ball or ball-marker is accidentally *moved* in the process of placing or replacing the ball, the ball or the ball-marker shall be replaced. There is no penalty provided the movement of the ball or the ball-marker is directly attributable to the specific act of placing or replacing the ball or removing the ball-marker. Otherwise, **the player shall incur a *penalty stroke*** under Rule 18-2a or 20-1.

b Lie of Ball to be Placed or Replaced Altered

If the original lie of a ball to be placed or replaced has been altered:

(i) except in a *hazard,* the ball shall be placed in the nearest lie most similar to the original lie which is not more than one club-length from the original lie, not nearer the *hole* and not in a *hazard*;

(ii) in a *water hazard*, the ball shall be placed in accordance with Clause (i) above, except that the ball must be placed in the *water hazard*;

(iii) in a *bunker*, the original lie shall be recreated as nearly as possible and the ball shall be placed in that lie.

c Spot Not Determinable

See **incident** involving Rule 20-3c on page 115

If it is impossible to determine the spot where the ball is to be placed or replaced:

(i) *through the green*, the ball shall be dropped as near as possible to the place where it lay but not in a *hazard* or on a *putting green*;

(ii) in a *hazard*, the ball shall be dropped in the *hazard* as near as possible to the place where it lay;

(iii) on the *putting green*, the ball shall be placed as near as possible to the place where it lay but not in a *hazard*.

d Ball Fails to Come to Rest on Spot

See **incident** involving Rule 20-3d on page 87

If a ball when placed fails to come to rest on the spot on which it was placed, it shall be replaced without penalty.

If it still fails to come to rest on that spot:

(i) except in a *hazard*, it shall be placed at the nearest spot where it can be placed at rest which is not nearer the *hole* and not in a *hazard*;

(ii) in a *hazard*, it shall be placed in the *hazard* at the nearest spot where it can be placed at rest which is not nearer the *hole*.

If a ball when placed comes to rest on the spot on which it is placed, and it subsequently *moves*, there is no penalty and the ball shall be played as it lies, unless the provisions of any other *Rule* apply.

PENALTY FOR BREACH OF RULE 20-1, -2 or -3: *Match play — Loss of hole; Stroke play — Two strokes.*

20-4 WHEN BALL DROPPED OR PLACED IS IN PLAY

If the player's *ball in play* has been lifted, it is again in play when dropped or placed.

A substituted ball becomes the *ball in play* when it has been dropped or placed.

(Ball incorrectly substituted — see Rule 15-1.)

(Lifting ball incorrectly substituted, dropped or placed — see Rule 20-6.)

20-5 PLAYING NEXT STROKE FROM WHERE PREVIOUS STROKE PLAYED

When, under the *Rules*, a player elects or is required to play his next *stroke* from where a previous *stroke* was played, he shall proceed as follows: if the *stroke* is to be played from the *teeing ground*, the ball to be played shall be played from anywhere within the *teeing ground* and may be teed; if the *stroke* is to be played from *through the green* or a *hazard*, it shall be dropped; if the *stroke* is to be played on the *putting green*, it shall be placed.

PENALTY FOR BREACH OF RULE 20-5: *Match play — Loss of hole; Stroke play — Two strokes.*

20-6 LIFTING BALL INCORRECTLY SUBSTITUTED, DROPPED OR PLACED

A ball incorrectly substituted, dropped or placed in a wrong place or otherwise not in accordance with the *Rules* but not played may be lifted, without penalty, and the player shall then proceed correctly.

20-7 PLAYING FROM WRONG PLACE

For a ball played from outside the *teeing ground* or from a wrong *teeing ground* — see Rule 11-4 and -5.

a Match Play

If a player plays a *stroke* with a ball which has been dropped or placed in a wrong place, **he shall lose the hole**.

b Stroke Play

See **incident** involving Rule 20-7b on page 84

If a *competitor* plays a *stroke* with his *ball in play* (i) which has been dropped or placed in a wrong place or (ii) which has been *moved* and not replaced in a case where the *Rules* require replacement, **he shall**, provided a serious breach has not occurred, **incur the penalty prescribed by the applicable *Rule*** and play out the hole with the ball.

If, after playing from a wrong place, a *competitor* becomes aware of that fact and believes that a serious breach may be involved, he may, provided he has not played a *stroke* from the next *teeing ground* or, in the case of the last hole of the round, left the *putting green*, declare that he will play out the hole with a second ball dropped or placed in accordance with the *Rules*. The *competitor* shall report the facts to the *Committee* before returning his score card; if he fails to do so, **he shall be disqualified**. The *Committee* shall determine whether a serious breach of the Rule occurred.

PLAYING FROM WRONG PLACE

If a player moves his ball-marker a putter head length to one side, he must remember to put it back before he putts. Otherwise, the player will be penalized for playing from a wrong place.

If so, the score with the second ball shall count and **the *competitor* shall add two *penalty strokes* to his score with that ball**.

If a serious breach has occurred and the *competitor* has failed to correct it as prescribed above, **he shall be disqualified**.

Note: If a *competitor* plays a second ball, *penalty strokes* incurred solely by playing the ball ruled not to count and *strokes* subsequently taken with that ball shall be disregarded.

RULE 20 INCIDENTS

At the 1984 Masters Tournament, Billy Casper was unaware or had momentarily forgotten that the method described in the Rules of Golf for dropping a ball had been changed that year. Casper used the old method, played his ball and was assessed one penalty stroke.

Casper had won the event in 1970 after a playoff with Gene Littler. The infraction he incurred for a wrong drop 14 years later had no appreciable effect on the tournament results or prize money awarded. Had he dropped properly, Casper would still have missed the cut.

On the first green at the Olympic Club during the first round of the 1998 U.S. Open, Mike Reid was replacing his ball when it slipped out of his hand. His ball fell onto and moved the coin that was marking its position. Reid inquired of the Rules official walking with the group and was told a penalty had not been incurred because the official believed Reid's action was "directly attributable" to the act of replacing his ball. Reid finished the round, returned his score card and went to the locker room.

When the incident was brought to the attention of senior Rules officials, it was determined that Reid's action was not "directly attributable to the specific act" of replacing his ball and that one penalty stroke should be added to his score as stipulated by Rules 20-1 and 18-2. Reid was not disqualified for returning a score card with a score lower than he had actually made because the official walking with his group had initially told him there was no penalty.

Because of this incident, "Directly attributable to the specific act" is now defined by Decision 20-1/15 and eliminates from consideration "accidental movement of the ball or the ball-marker which occurs before or after this specific act, such as dropping the ball or ball-marker, regardless of the height from which it was dropped…"

The infraction for lifting an opponent's ball without authorization can be deadly in match play. In the 1988 U.S. Amateur Championship, which was played at The Cascades in Hot Springs, VA, Danny Yates mistook his opponent's ball for his own and lifted it without permission. The mistake took place on the 21st hole of the 36-hole final round. The one stroke penalty under Rule 18-3b resulted in Yates losing the hole to Eric Meeks, who eventually won the match and the championship, 7 and 6.

Hale Irwin learned at the 1995 Senior Tour Championship that trying to do the right thing by correcting an error can sometimes compound an infraction and add to the resulting penalty.

At The Dunes Club in Myrtle Beach, Irwin erroneously replaced his ball on the 16th putting green in front of his fellow-competitor's marker. After putting, Irwin realized his mistake and, believing he needed to correct his error, lifted his ball, replaced it in front of his marker and finished the hole.

His penalty totaled four strokes. When Irwin replaced his ball in front of his fellow-competitor's marker and putted, he played from a wrong place and incurred a two-stroke penalty under Rule 16-1b. When he subsequently lifted his ball from where it lay without marking its position and did not replace it, he also incurred the general penalty of two strokes under Rule 20-1.

RULE 21 CLEANING BALL

See **incident** involving Rule 21 below

A ball on the *putting green* may be cleaned when lifted under Rule l6-1b. Elsewhere, a ball may be cleaned when lifted except when it has been lifted:

a. To determine if it is unfit for play (Rule 5-3);

b. For identification (Rule 12-2), in which case it may be cleaned only to the extent necessary for identification; or

c. Because it is interfering with or assisting play (Rule 22).

If a player cleans his ball during play of a hole except as provided in this Rule, **he shall incur a penalty of one stroke** and the ball, if lifted, shall be replaced.

If a player who is required to replace a ball fails to do so, **he shall incur the penalty** for breach of Rule 20-3a, but no additional penalty under Rule 21 shall be applied.

Exception: If a player incurs a penalty for failing to act in accordance with Rule 5-3, 12-2 or 22, no additional penalty under Rule 21 shall be applied.

RULE 21 INCIDENT

During the 1999 U.S. Open at Pinehurst — six holes after the incident described under Rule 22 (see page 87) — Scott Hoch holed his bunker shot at the par-4 12th. During the clamor, the walking official looked up to see two senior Rules officials motioning him to come over.

The senior officials reported that a spectator had alleged that Hoch's ball was mistakenly cleaned when lifted for interference at the 6th hole. Rule 22 permits the lifting of a ball that interferes with or assists the play of another player. Under such circumstances, except on the putting green, the ball may not be cleaned when lifted under Rule 22.

The senior officials asked the walking official if he could confirm whether Hoch's ball had been cleaned when lifted from the greenside rough. The walking official stated that his attention had been primarily focused on the lifting and replacing procedures and he was unaware of any cleaning violation.

It was decided to ask Hoch after he finished the round but before he returned his score card. When the inquiry was made Hoch replied that he did not recall since the incident had occurred two hours before. Hoch's caddie also said he did not recall. Parnevik and Jones said they were not watching and could not say.

Since there was no evidence to the contrary, Hoch was found to have acted properly and he began the second round just four shots out of the lead.

RULE 22

BALL INTERFERING WITH OR ASSISTING PLAY

See **incident** involving Rule 22 on page 87

Any player may:
a. Lift his ball if he considers that the ball might assist any other player or
b. Have any other ball lifted if he considers that the ball might interfere with his play or assist the play of any other player, but this may not be done while another ball is in motion. In stroke play, a player required to lift his ball may play first rather than lift. A ball lifted under this Rule shall be replaced.

PENALTY FOR BREACH OF RULE: *Match play — Loss of hole; Stroke play — Two strokes.*

Note: Except on the *putting green*, the ball may not be cleaned when lifted under this Rule — see Rule 21.

RULE 22 INCIDENT

Because golf is played on the largest playing field of any sport, it's rare when one ball touches another. The insular nature of golf at its highest level makes such an occurrence even more bizarre at major championships.

Jesper Parnevik and Scott Hoch found themselves in such a predicament just off the 6th green at Pinehurst No.2 during the 1999 U.S. Open. Fortunately, the procedure in such a situation is concise.

The shortest Rule in the book, Rule 22 allows any player to lift his ball if he believes it will assist another player, or have any ball lifted that might interfere with his play or assist any other player. Except on the putting green, a ball lifted under this Rule may not be cleaned.

Hoch and Parnevik both played just to the left side of the green at this 222-yard par 3. It was difficult from the tee to discern whether the balls were on the fringe of the green or in the rough. Their fellow-competitor's ball, that of Steve Jones, was visible on the green. Upon arriving greenside, they found that the balls were touching one another and lay about three inches off the fringe in the Bermuda grass rough. Both balls were held slightly off the ground by the stiff nature of the grass. Because Hoch's ball was closer to the hole, it was necessary that it be lifted in order for Parnevik to play his shot.

Before Hoch lifted his ball, the walking Rules official with the group closely inspected the lie of both balls to be certain 1) that Hoch, upon replacing his ball after Parnevik's stroke, would be afforded the same lie or if that were not possible, a most similar lie; and 2) that Parnevik's ball could be accurately replaced should it move when Hoch lifted his ball.

As anticipated, when Hoch lifted his ball, Parnevik's moved an inch closer to the hole. Under the Rules official's watchful eye, Parnevik attempted to replace his ball in its original location. However, the supporting nature of the Bermuda grass could not be reintroduced and Parnevik's ball sunk a littler deeper into the rough than its original position. Under the Rules, it doesn't matter if the movement is vertical or horizontal. The ball could not be replaced in its original position so that it would remain at rest.

Rule 20-3 covers such a situation by stating that if a ball, when placed or replaced, fails to come to rest on that spot it shall be replaced. If it again fails to remain at rest, it must be placed at the nearest spot where it can be placed at rest which is not nearer the hole and not in a hazard.

Therefore, Parnevik found another spot that was nearest to the original position where the ball would remain at rest. He chipped onto the green and in doing so altered Hoch's lie.

In this case, Hoch was entitled to the lie that his shot afforded him. Since his lie had been altered, he found the nearest lie most similar to his original lie within one club-length and placed his ball. Then he chipped in for a birdie two.

All of this was under the discerning eyes of both the walking Rules official and a Rules rover who was monitoring the group's pace of play. Parnevik and Jones finished the hole and the group went to the 7th tee. See Rule 21 for a continuation of this incident.

RULE 23   LOOSE IMPEDIMENTS

DEFINITIONS

"Loose impediments" are natural objects such as stones, leaves, twigs, branches and the like, dung, worms and insects and casts or heaps made by them, provided they are not fixed or growing, are not solidly embedded and do not adhere to the ball.

Sand and loose soil are *loose impediments* on the *putting green* but not elsewhere.

Snow and natural ice, other than frost, are either *casual water* or *loose impediments*, at the option of the player. Manufactured ice is an *obstruction*.

Dew and frost are not *loose impediments*.

23-1 RELIEF

Except when both the *loose impediment* and the ball lie in or touch the same *hazard*, any *loose impediment* may be removed without penalty. If the ball *moves*, see Rule 18-2c.

When a ball is in motion, a *loose impediment* which might influence the movement of the ball shall not be removed.

See **incident** involving Rule 23-1 on page 89

A player is entitled to remove any loose impediment without penalty, except when both the loose impediment and the player's ball lie in or touch the same hazard.

Loose impediments are natural objects that come in all shapes and sizes. At the 1999 Phoenix Open, Tiger Woods learned that a player can receive assistance in removing a large loose impediment. Details of this incident can be reviewed below.

PENALTY FOR BREACH OF RULE: *Match play — Loss of hole; Stroke play — Two strokes.*
(Searching for ball in *hazard* — see Rule 12-1.)
(Touching *line of putt* — see Rule 16-1a.)

RULE 23 INCIDENT

The Rules of Golf permitted Tiger Woods to gain assistance from his substantial gallery in moving a loose impediment during the 1999 Phoenix Open.

During the final round, Woods' drive from the 13th tee traveled 360 yards before finishing in the desert just off the left side of the fairway. The ball stopped about two feet directly behind a boulder that was roughly four feet wide, two feet high and two feet thick. The rock was too heavy for Woods to move by himself, and his ball was too close to it to play over or around. Without moving the rock, his best option would have been to play sideways into the fairway.

With 225 yards to the putting green, Woods was not inclined to pitch out without first knowing what his options were with regard to the rock.

PGA Tour Rules Official Orlando Pope appeared at the scene. With a glimmer of a smile on his face, Woods kicked the rock and asked, "... It's not a pebble but is it a loose impediment?"

The definition within the Rules of Golf states that loose impediments are natural objects that are not fixed or growing, not solidly embedded and do not adhere to the ball. There is no reference to size or weight.

Decision 23-1/2 states that stones of any size are loose impediments and may be removed, as long as they are not solidly embedded and their removal does not unduly delay play.

Pope replied, "It's readily movable if you have people who can move it real quick."

"Really?" Woods responded to the revelation quietly.

Then Pope added in an inquiring tone, "But it kind of looks embedded to me."

"It's embedded?" Woods asked as they both stepped back to look.

Pope decided the stone was just lying on the desert floor and was not solidly embedded. He also knew that Decision 23-1/3 specifically permits spectators, caddies, fellow-competitors, essentially anyone to assist in removing a large loose impediment.

Several men rolled the stone out of Woods' line of play as others watched and cheered. Following the removal, Woods shook each man's hand and then played his shot directly toward the green, where it finished in the right greenside bunker.

Golf's stars have always enjoyed and suffered the effects of their large galleries. Bobby Jones had to be protected by Marines when he completed his Grand Slam at Merion in 1930. Sam Snead, Arnold Palmer and Jack Nicklaus often had errant shots stopped by those who followed them.

In addition to the times they were helped, imagine the number of times that Jones, Snead, Palmer, Nicklaus and Woods have been distracted by a movement or noise coming from the galleries, photographers, reporters and security officers that follow them. It has never been the function of the Rules of Golf to try to equalize these varied possibilities.

RULE **24**

OBSTRUCTIONS

DEFINITIONS

The *"nearest point of relief"* is the reference point for taking relief without penalty from interference by an immovable *obstruction* (Rule 24-2), an *abnormal ground condition* (Rule 25-1) or a *wrong putting green* (see Rule 25-3).

It is the point on the *course*, nearest to where the ball lies, which is not nearer the *hole* and at which, if the ball were so positioned, no interference (as defined) would exist.

Note: The player should determine his *nearest point of relief* by using the club with which he expects to play his next *stroke* to simulate the *address* position and swing for such *stroke*.

An *"obstruction"* is anything artificial, including the artificial surfaces and sides of roads and paths and manufactured ice, except:

a. Objects defining *out of bounds*, such as walls, fences, stakes and railings;

b. Any part of an immovable artificial object which is *out of bounds*; and

c. Any construction declared by the *Committee* to be an integral part of the *course*.

An *obstruction* is a movable *obstruction* if it may be moved without unreasonable effort, without unduly delaying play and without causing damage. Otherwise, it is an immovable *obstruction*.

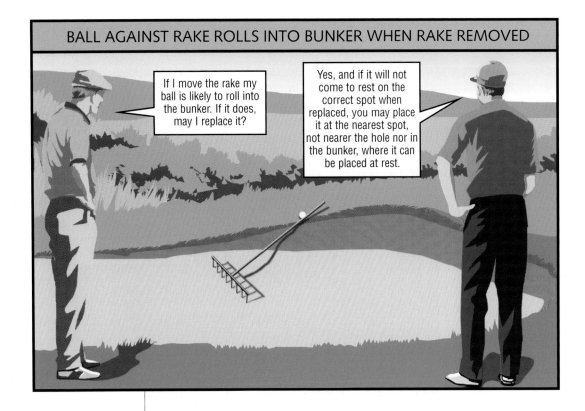

Note: The *Committee* may make a Local Rule declaring a movable *obstruction* to be an immovable *obstruction*.

24-1 MOVABLE OBSTRUCTION

See **incident** involving Rule 24-1 on page 96

A player may obtain relief from a movable *obstruction* as follows:
a. If the ball does not lie in or on the *obstruction*, the *obstruction* may be removed. If the ball *moves*, it shall be replaced, and there is no penalty provided that the movement of the ball is directly attributable to the removal of the *obstruction*. Otherwise, Rule 18-2a applies.
b. If the ball lies in or on the *obstruction*, the ball may be lifted, without penalty, and the *obstruction* removed. The ball shall *through the green* or in a *hazard* be dropped, or on the *putting green* be placed, as near as possible to the spot directly under the place where the ball lay in or on the *obstruction*, but not nearer the *hole*.

The ball may be cleaned when lifted under Rule 24-1.

When a ball is in motion, an *obstruction* which might influence the movement of the ball, other than an attended *flagstick* or *equipment* of the players, shall not be removed.
(Exerting influence on the ball — see Rule 1-2.)
Note: If a ball to be dropped or placed under this Rule is not immediately recoverable, another ball may be substituted.

24-2 IMMOVABLE OBSTRUCTION
a Interference
Interference by an immovable *obstruction* occurs when a ball lies in or on the *obstruction*, or so close to the *obstruction* that the *obstruction* interferes

with the player's *stance* or the area of his intended swing. If the player's ball lies on the *putting green*, interference also occurs if an immovable *obstruction* on the *putting green* intervenes on his *line of putt*. Otherwise, intervention on the *line of play* is not, of itself, interference under this Rule.

b Relief

Except when the ball is in a *water hazard* or a *lateral water hazard*, a player may obtain relief from interference by an immovable *obstruction*, without penalty, as follows:

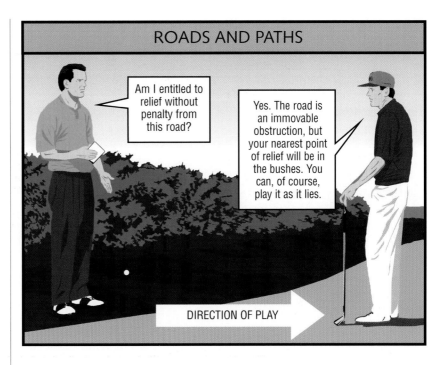

See **incident** involving Rule 24-2b on page 96

(i) ***Through the Green:*** If the ball lies *through the green*, the *nearest point of relief* shall be determined which is not in a *hazard* or on a *putting green*. The player shall lift the ball and drop it within one club-length of and not nearer the *hole* than the *nearest point of relief*, on a part of the *course* which avoids interference (as defined) by the immovable *obstruction* and is not in a *hazard* or on a *putting green*.

(ii) **In a *Bunker*:** If the ball is in a *bunker*, the player shall lift and drop the ball in accordance with Clause (i) above, except that the *nearest point*

of relief must be in the bunker and the ball must be dropped in the bunker.

(iii) **On the Putting Green**: If the ball lies on the putting green, the player shall lift the ball and place it at the nearest point of relief which is not in a hazard. The nearest point of relief may be off the putting green.

The ball may be cleaned when lifted under Rule 24-2b.

(Ball rolling to a position where there is interference by the condition from which relief was taken — see Rule 20-2c(v).)

When the Committee declares an immovable obstruction to be an integral part of the course, in this case the road behind the 17th green of the Old Course at St Andrews, relief without penalty is not available.

NO RELIEF WITHOUT PENALTY IN WATER HAZARD

Although my ball is in the hazard it is playable, except that pipe interferes with my swing. May I take free relief?

I'm afraid not. Your ball is in a water hazard and there is no free relief from an immovable obstruction in this situation. You will have to play it or proceed under the Water Hazard Rule.

BALL ON BRIDGE ABOVE HAZARD

The ball is in the water hazard because the margins of a water hazard are deemed to extend vertically upwards. The bridge is an immovable obstruction but there is no relief without penalty from an immovable obstruction when the ball lies in or touches a water hazard. If the ball is played from the bridge the club may be grounded.

95

RELIEF SITUATIONS AND PROCEDURE

See **incident** involving the exception to Rule 24-2b below

Exception: A player may not obtain relief under Rule 24–2b if (a) it is clearly unreasonable for him to play a *stroke* because of interference by anything other than an immovable *obstruction* or (b) interference by an immovable *obstruction* would occur only through use of an unnecessarily abnormal *stance*, swing or direction of play.

Note 1: If a ball is in a *water hazard* (including a *lateral water hazard*), the player is not entitled to relief without penalty from interference by an immovable *obstruction*. The player shall play the ball as it lies or proceed under Rule 26-1.

Note 2: If a ball to be dropped or placed under this Rule is not immediately recoverable, another ball may be substituted.

Note 3: The *Committee* may make a Local Rule stating that the player must determine the *nearest point of relief* without crossing over, through or under the *obstruction*.

c Ball lost

It is a question of fact whether a ball lost after having been struck toward an immovable *obstruction* is lost in the *obstruction*. In order to treat the ball as lost in the *obstruction*, there must be reasonable evidence to that effect. In the absence of such evidence, the ball must be treated as a *lost ball* and Rule 27 applies.

If a ball is *lost* in an immovable *obstruction*, the spot where the ball last entered the *obstruction* shall be determined and, for the purpose of applying this Rule, the ball shall be deemed to lie at this spot.

(i)   *Through the Green*: If the ball last entered the immovable *obstruction* at a spot *through the green*, the player may substitute another ball without penalty and take relief as prescribed in Rule 24-2b(i).

(ii) **In a *Bunker*:** If the ball last entered the immovable *obstruction* at a spot in a *bunker*, the player may substitute another ball without penalty and take relief as prescribed in Rule 24-2b(ii).

(iii) **In a *Water Hazard* (including a *Lateral Water Hazard*):** If the ball last entered the immovable *obstruction* at a spot in a *water hazard*, the player is not entitled to relief without penalty. The player shall proceed under Rule 26-1.

(iv) **On the *Putting Green*:** If the ball last entered the immovable *obstruction* at a spot on the *putting green*, the player may substitute another ball without penalty and take relief as prescribed in Rule 24-2b(iii).

PENALTY FOR BREACH OF RULE: *Match play — Loss of hole; Stroke play — Two strokes.*

RULE 24 INCIDENTS

Since 1744, the basic tenets of the Rules have been to play the course as you find it, the ball as it lies and, if you are unsure of the proper procedure, to do what is fair. Harry Bradshaw held true to this spirit at the 1949 British Open.

Having shot a stunning first round 68 over Royal St. George's on the coast of the English Channel, Bradshaw was tied with Roberto De

Vicenzo one stroke behind Jimmy Adams. However, playing the 5th hole during the second round, Bradshaw's ball rolled into a littered beer bottle from which the neck had been broken.

Rather than requesting a ruling for the relief to which he was entitled, Bradshaw determined on his own that he must play the ball as it lay. He took out his sand wedge and made a swing, which shattered the bottle and moved the ball slightly forward. He took a double bogey six.

The result of his playing out of this movable obstruction was that Bradshaw ultimately tied Bobby Locke of South Africa at 283. In the resulting 36-hole playoff, Locke bested Bradshaw, 136-147, to win the first of Locke's four British Open Championships.

Under Rule 24-1, because Bradshaw's ball was in a movable obstruction, the ball could have been lifted and cleaned without penalty, the bottle removed and the ball dropped as nearly as possible to the spot directly under the place where the ball lay when it was in the bottle.

In choosing to take relief from an immovable obstruction, the ball must be dropped in a place that avoids interference by the immovable obstruction. Full relief must be taken. Payne Stewart learned this lesson in 1993 during the PGA Tour's annual stop in San Diego.

In taking relief from a cart path, Stewart dropped his ball in a place where, after taking his stance, the heel of his right shoe was still on the cart path from which he was taking relief. The television broadcast showed the infraction clearly and Stewart was penalized two strokes for not taking complete relief from the immovable obstruction.

The exception to Rule 24-2 states clearly that a player may not obtain relief under this Rule if interference would only occur through the use of an abnormal stance, swing or direction of play. This is one of the places in the Rules where a referee's judgment is called upon, as David Frost learned during the final round of the 1999 British Open at Carnoustie.

Playing with Justin Leonard in the penultimate group, Frost's drive at the second hole was a low hook into the high rough. Near the area where he would stand to play the ball was a road. Frost argued to the attending Rules official that in order to play the ball, which was below his feet, he would have to widen his stance to such an extent that he would be standing on the road and, therefore, entitled to relief from an immovable obstruction.

The referee did not accept the argument and told Frost that such a play was not reasonable. It was the referee's judgment that had the road not been there, Frost would not have used a stance that would place his left foot on the road. With the final pairing waiting on the tee, time ticked away as confirmation of the referee's decision was requested over the radio. It was deemed final, and Frost played the ball as it lay.

In such a situation, the referee must consider how the player would attempt the shot if the obstruction in question were not present. In a stroke play situation such as this one, the Rules are there to protect the field and prevent an unfair advantage of one player over all the others.

When the Committee declares an obstruction an integral part of the golf course, it eliminates any argument because there is no free relief. The most famous example of this is the Road Hole at the Old Course in St Andrews. When a ball lies upon this road immediately to the right of the green, it must be played as it lies. As its name signals, the road has always been the most important element of the 17th hole, and to allow relief would eliminate one of its essential obstacles. Thus, it is an integral part of the golf course.

RULE 25 ABNORMAL GROUND CONDITIONS, EMBEDDED BALL AND WRONG PUTTING GREEN

DEFINITIONS

An *"abnormal ground condition"* is any *casual water, ground under repair* or a hole, cast or runway on the *course* made by a *burrowing animal*, a reptile or a bird.

A *"burrowing animal"* is an animal that makes a hole for habitation or shelter, such as a rabbit, mole, groung hog, gopher or salamander.

Note: A hole made by a non-*burrowing animal*, such as a dog, is not an *abnormal ground condition* unless marked or declared as *ground under repair*.

"Casual water" is any temporary accumulation of water on the *course* which is visible before or after the player takes his *stance* and is not in a *water hazard*. Snow and natural ice, other than frost, are *casual water* or *loose impediments*, at the option of the player. Manufactured ice is an *obstruction*. Dew and frost are not *casual water*. A ball is in *casual water* when it lies in or any part of it touches the *casual water*.

A fallen tree still attached to its stump is not ground under repair., but it can be so declared by the Committee.

A rut made by a tractor is not ground under repair, but the Committee would be justified in declaring a deep rut to be ground under repair.

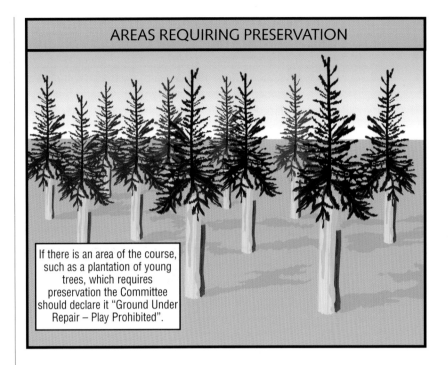

AREAS REQUIRING PRESERVATION

If there is an area of the course, such as a plantation of young trees, which requires preservation the Committee should declare it "Ground Under Repair – Play Prohibited".

"*Ground under repair*" is any part of the *course* so marked by order of the *Committee* or so declared by its authorised representative. It includes material piled for removal and a hole made by a greenkeeper, even if not so marked.

All ground and any grass, bush, tree or other growing thing within the *ground under repair* is part of the *ground under repair*. The margin of *ground under repair* extends vertically downwards, but not upwards. Stakes and lines defining *ground under repair* are in such ground. Such stakes are *obstructions*. A ball is in *ground under repair* when it lies in or any part of it touches the *ground under repair*.

Note 1: Grass cuttings and other material left on the *course* which have been abandoned and are not intended to be removed are not *ground under repair* unless so marked.

Note 2: The *Committee* may make a Local Rule prohibiting play from *ground under repair* or an environmentally-sensitive area which has been defined as *ground under repair*.

The "*nearest point of relief*" is the reference point for taking relief without penalty from interference by an immovable *obstruction* (Rule 24-2), an *abnormal ground condition* (Rule 25-1) or a *wrong putting green* (Rule 25-3).

It is the point on the *course*, nearest to where the ball lies, which is not nearer the *hole* and at which, if the ball were so positioned, no interference (as defined) would exist.

Note: The player should determine his *nearest point of relief* by using the club with which he expects to play his next *stroke* to simulate the address position and swing for such stroke.

A "*wrong putting green*" is any *putting green* other than that of the hole being played. Unless otherwise prescribed by the *Committee*, this term includes a practice *putting green* or pitching green on the *course*.

25-1 ABNORMAL GROUND CONDITION

a Interference

Interference by an *abnormal ground condition* occurs when a ball lies in or touches the condition or when such a condition interferes with the player's *stance* or the area of his intended swing. If the player's ball lies on the *putting green*, interference also occurs if such condition on the *putting green* intervenes on his *line of putt*. Otherwise, intervention on the *line of play* is not, of itself, interference under this Rule.

Note: The *Committee* may make a Local Rule denying the player relief from interference with his *stance* by an *abnormal ground condition*.

b Relief

Except when the ball is in a *water hazard* or a *lateral water hazard*, a player may obtain relief from interference by an *abnormal ground condition* as follows:

See **incident** involving Rule 25-1b on page 105

(i)   ***Through the Green:*** If the ball lies *through the green*, the *nearest point of relief* shall be determined which is not in a *hazard* or on a *putting green*. The player shall lift the ball and drop it without penalty within one club-length of and not nearer the *hole* than the *nearest point of relief*, on a part of the *course* which avoids interference (as defined) by the condition and is not in a *hazard* or on a *putting green*.

(ii)   **In a *Bunker*:** If the ball is in a *bunker*, the player shall lift and drop the ball either:
(a) Without penalty, in accordance with Clause (i) above, except that the *nearest point of relief* must be in the *bunker* and the ball must be dropped in the *bunker*, or if complete relief is impossible, in the *bunker* as near as possible to the spot where the ball lay, but not nearer the *hole*, on a part of the *course* which affords maximum available relief from the condition; or
(b) **Under penalty of one stroke**, outside the *bunker* keeping the point where the ball lay directly between the *hole* and the spot on which the ball is dropped, with no limit to how far behind the *bunker* the ball may be dropped.

(iii) **On the *Putting Green*:** If the ball lies on the *putting green*, the player shall lift the ball and place it without penalty at the *nearest point of relief* which is not in a *hazard*, or if complete relief is impossible, at the nearest position to where it lay which affords maximum available relief from the condition, but not nearer the *hole* nor in a *hazard*. The *nearest point of relief* or maximum available relief may be off the *putting green*.

The ball may be cleaned when lifted under Rule 25-1b.

(Ball rolling to a position where there is interference by the condition from which relief was taken – see Rule 20-2c(v).)

Exception: A player may not obtain relief under Rule 25-1b if (a) it is clearly unreasonable for him to play a *stroke* because of interference by anything other than a condition covered by Rule 25–1a or (b) interference by such a condition would occur only through use of an unnecessarily abnormal *stance*, swing or direction of play.

Note 1: If a ball is in a *water hazard* (including a *lateral water hazard*), the player is not entitled to relief without penalty from interference by an

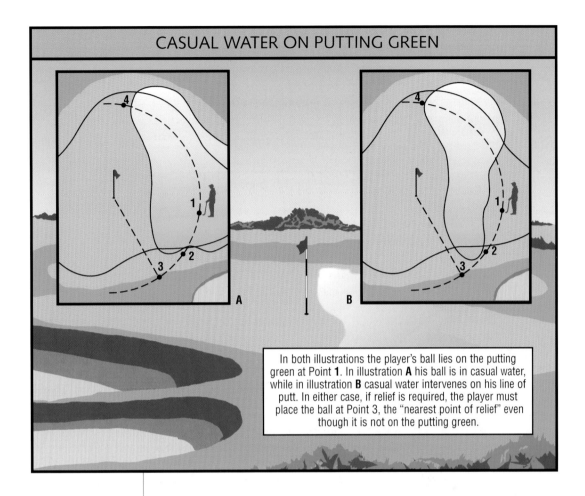

CASUAL WATER ON PUTTING GREEN

In both illustrations the player's ball lies on the putting green at Point **1**. In illustration **A** his ball is in casual water, while in illustration **B** casual water intervenes on his line of putt. In either case, if relief is required, the player must place the ball at Point 3, the "nearest point of relief" even though it is not on the putting green.

abnormal ground condition. The player shall play the ball as it lies (unless prohibited by Local Rule) or proceed under Rule 26-1.

Note 2: If a ball to be dropped or placed under this Rule is not immediately recoverable, another ball may be substituted.

c Ball Lost

It is a question of fact whether a ball *lost* after having been struck toward an *abnormal ground condition* is *lost* in such condition. In order to treat the ball as *lost* in the abnormal ground condition, there must be reasonable evidence to that effect. In the absence of such evidence, the ball must be treated as a *lost ball* and Rule 27 applies.

   If a ball is *lost* in an *abnormal ground condition*, the spot where the ball last entered the condition shall be determined and, for the purposes of applying this Rule, the ball shall be deemed to lie at this spot.

(i)   ***Through the Green:*** If the ball last entered the *abnormal ground condition* at a spot *through the green*, the player may substitute another ball without penalty and take relief as prescribed in Rule 25-1b(i).

See **incident** involving Rule 25-1c on page 105

(ii) **In a *Bunker*:** If the ball last entered the *abnormal ground condition* at a spot in a *bunker*, the player may substitute another ball without penalty and take relief as prescribed in Rule 25-1b(ii).

101

(iii) **In a *Water Hazard* (including a *Lateral Water Hazard*):** If the ball last entered the *abnormal ground condition* at a spot in a *water hazard*, the player is not entitled to relief without penalty. The player shall proceed under Rule 26-1.

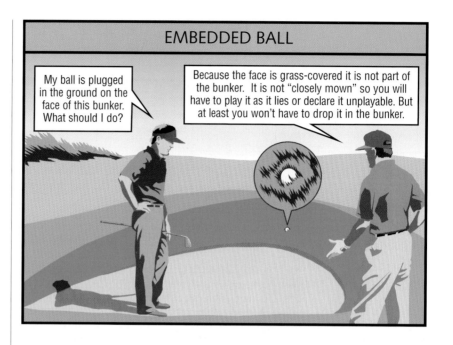

(iv) **On the *Putting Green*:** If the ball last entered the *abnormal ground condition* at a spot on the *putting green*, the player may substitute another ball without penalty and take relief as prescribed in Rule 25-1b(iii).

25-2 EMBEDDED BALL

A ball embedded in its own pitch-mark in the ground in any closely-mown area *through the green* may be lifted, cleaned and dropped, without penalty, as near as possible to the spot where it lay but not nearer the *hole*. The ball when dropped must first strike a part of the *course through the green*.

"Closely-mown area" means any area of the *course*, including paths through the rough, cut to fairway height or less.

25-3 WRONG PUTTING GREEN

a Interference

Interference by a *wrong putting green* occurs when a ball is on the *wrong putting green*.

Interference to a player's *stance* or the area of his intended swing is not, of itself, interference under this Rule.

b Relief

See **incident** involving Rule 25-3 on page 105

If a player has interference by a *wrong putting green*, the player must take relief, without penalty, as follows:

The *nearest point of relief* shall be determined which is not in a *hazard* or on a *putting green*. The player shall lift the ball and drop it within one club-length of and not nearer the *hole* than the *nearest point of relief*, on a part of the *course* which avoids interference (as defined) by the *wrong putting green* and is not in a *hazard* or on a *putting green*. The ball may be cleaned when so lifted.

PENALTY FOR BREACH OF RULE: *Match play — Loss of hole; Stroke play — Two strokes.*

RULE 25 INCIDENTS

Patty Sheehan was able to use Rule 25 to aid her in tying Juli Inkster during regulation play of the 1992 U.S. Women's Open. A sudden downpour across the hills of western Pennsylvania suspended play at Oakmont Country Club during the final round. Once play resumed, casual water was present in various places on the course.

At the final hole, Sheehan needed a birdie three to tie Inkster and force a playoff. Sheehan's drive was not promising. Her ball drifted to the right and settled in the high, wet rough.

Sheehan was faced with a mid-iron shot from wet, U.S. Women's Open rough that had to stop near the hole on an undulating green that is guarded front right and left by large bunkers.

Upon taking her stance water was visible that fell within the definition of casual water as "any temporary accumulation of water on the course which is visible before or after the player takes his stance and is not in a water hazard."

Though Sheehan's ball was off the fairway in the rough, the Rules of Golf make no distinction between rough and fairway as regards abnormal ground conditions. Directions for relief under Rule 25-1 state simply "if the ball lies through the green, the nearest point of relief shall be determined which is not in a hazard or on a putting green." Once that point is found, the player must drop the ball within one club-length and no nearer the hole.

In determining her nearest point of relief plus the one club-length,

Sheehan discovered that her dropping point was in the fairway. Under the watchful eyes of a walking Rules official and an observer, she lifted the ball from the rough and appropriately dropped it in the fairway. Her second shot landed short of the putting green and ran onto the green. The ball finished close enough that Sheehan was able to make the birdie putt and tie Inkster after 72 holes.

In the following day's 18-hole playoff, Sheehan scored 72 to Inkster's 74 and won the first of her two U.S. Women's Open Championships.

During the second round of The Players Championship in 1999, marshals at the 18th green watched Greg Norman's ball roll into a hole made by a burrowing animal. When a ball is lost in an abnormal ground condition, there must be reasonable evidence to that effect. Suspecting that the ball might have gone into the burrowing animal hole is not good enough and, indeed, the Australian started to put his hand into the hole to determine if the ball was there.

The attending official told Norman that the marshals' statements that they had seen the ball go into the burrowing animal hole consti-tuted reasonable evidence. Therefore, he was entitled to relief without penalty, and it was not necessary to reach into the hole in order to retrieve the ball.

A rare incidence of playing from a wrong putting green took place at the 1990 U.S. Senior Open at Ridgewood Country Club in Paramus, NJ.

Ridgewood has 27 holes. The third nine was out of play for the championship but not out of bounds. From the second tee, a player hooked his drive onto a green that is part of the third nine. From that green, the competitor played back to the second hole of the competi-tive course.

An observant marshal queried the player's procedure with a Rules official, and the player was penalized two strokes under Rule 25-3. It is important to note that had the player's ball been on the fringe of the putting green requiring a stance, by either foot, on the wrong putting green, the player would have been required to play the ball as it lay and would have incurred no penalty.

RULE **26**

WATER HAZARDS
(INCLUDING LATERAL WATER HAZARDS)

DEFINITIONS

A "*water hazard*" is any sea, lake, pond, river, ditch, surface drainage ditch or other open water course (whether or not containing water) and anything of a similar nature.

All ground or water within the margin of a *water hazard* is part of the *water hazard*. The margin of a *water hazard* extends vertically upwards and downwards. Stakes and lines defining the margins of *water hazards* are in the *hazards*. Such stakes are *obstructions*. A ball is in a *water hazard* when it lies in or any part of it touches the *water hazard*.

Note 1: *Water hazards* (other than *lateral water hazards*) should be defined by yellow stakes or lines.

Note 2: The *Committee* may make a Local Rule prohibiting play from an environmentally-sensitive area which has been defined as a *water hazard*.

A "*lateral water hazard*" is a *water hazard* or that part of a *water hazard* so situated that it is not possible or is deemed by the *Committee* to be impracticable to drop a ball behind the *water hazard* in accordance with Rule 26-1b.

That part of a *water hazard* to be played as a *lateral water hazard* should be distinctively marked. A ball is in a *lateral water hazard* when it lies in or any part of it touches the *lateral water hazard*.

Note 1: *Lateral water hazards* should be defined by red stakes or lines.

Note 2: The *Committee* may make a Local Rule prohibiting play from an environmentally-sensitive area which has been defined as a *lateral water hazard*.

Note 3: The *Committee* may define a *lateral water hazard* as a *water hazard*.

26-1 BALL IN WATER HAZARD

It is a question of fact whether a ball lost after having been struck toward a *water hazard* is lost inside or outside the *hazard*. In order to treat the ball as lost in the *hazard*, there must be reasonable evidence that the ball lodged in it. In the absence of such evidence, the ball must be treated as a *lost ball* and Rule 27 applies.

If a ball is in or is lost in a *water hazard* (whether the ball lies in water or not), the player may **under penalty of one stroke:**

a. Play a ball as nearly as possible at the spot from which the original ball was last played (see Rule 20-5); or

REASONABLE EVIDENCE BALL IN WATER HAZARD

Jean Van de Velde's difficulty with the Barry Burn at the 72nd hole of the 1999 British Open resulted in a three-way playoff for the championship. See the details of his unfortunate brush with Rule 26-1 in the story on page 111.

See **incident** involving Rule 26-1b on page 111

b. Drop a ball behind the *water hazard*, keeping the point at which the original ball last crossed the margin of the *water hazard* directly between the *hole* and the spot on which the ball is dropped, with no limit to how far behind the *water hazard* the ball may be dropped; or

c. As additional options available only if the ball last crossed the margin of a *lateral water hazard*, drop a ball outside the *water hazard* within two club-lengths of and not nearer the *hole* than (i) the point where the original ball last crossed the margin of the *water hazard* or (ii) a point on the opposite margin of the *water hazard* equidistant from the *hole*.

The ball may be cleaned when lifted under this Rule.

(Ball moving in water in a *water hazard* — see Rule 14-6.)

26-2 BALL PLAYED WITHIN WATER HAZARD
a Ball Comes to Rest in the Hazard

If a ball played from within a *water hazard* comes to rest in the same *hazard* after the *stroke*, the player may:

(i)   proceed under Rule 26-1; or

(ii)   **under penalty of one stroke**, play a ball as nearly as possible at the spot from which the last *stroke* from outside the *hazard* was played (see Rule 20-5).

If the player proceeds under Rule 26-1a, he may elect not to play the dropped ball. If he so elects, he may:

a. Proceed under Rule 26-1b, **adding the additional penalty of one stroke** prescribed by that Rule; or

b. Proceed under Rule 26-1c, if applicable, **adding the additional penalty of one stroke** prescribed by that Rule; or

c. **Add an additional penalty of one stroke** and play a ball as nearly as possible at the spot from which the last *stroke* from outside the *hazard* was played (see Rule 20-5).

BALL CROSSING MARGIN OF WATER HAZARD

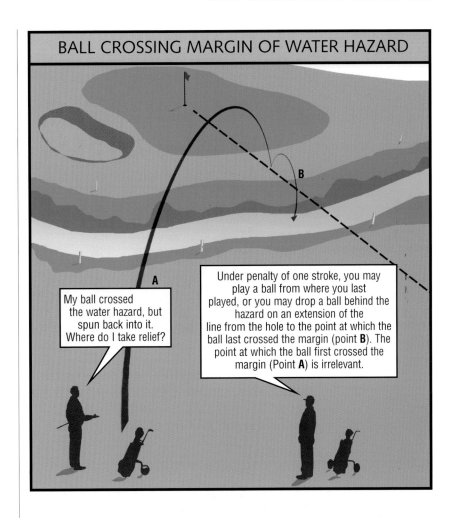

My ball crossed the water hazard, but spun back into it. Where do I take relief?

Under penalty of one stroke, you may play a ball from where you last played, or you may drop a ball behind the hazard on an extension of the line from the hole to the point at which the ball last crossed the margin (point **B**). The point at which the ball first crossed the margin (Point **A**) is irrelevant.

RELIEF FROM LATERAL WATER HAZARD

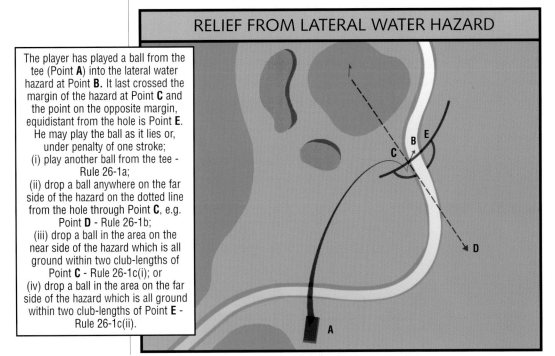

The player has played a ball from the tee (Point **A**) into the lateral water hazard at Point **B**. It last crossed the margin of the hazard at Point **C** and the point on the opposite margin, equidistant from the hole is Point **E**. He may play the ball as it lies or, under penalty of one stroke;
(i) play another ball from the tee - Rule 26-1a;
(ii) drop a ball anywhere on the far side of the hazard on the dotted line from the hole through Point **C**, e.g. Point **D** - Rule 26-1b;
(iii) drop a ball in the area on the near side of the hazard which is all ground within two club-lengths of Point **C** - Rule 26-1c(i); or
(iv) drop a ball in the area on the far side of the hazard which is all ground within two club-lengths of Point **E** - Rule 26-1c(ii).

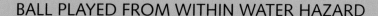

BALL PLAYED FROM WITHIN WATER HAZARD

The player's tee shot at a par 3 hole comes to rest in a water hazard. He plays from the hazard, but fails to get his ball out. He may play the ball as it lies or, under penalty of one stroke:
(i) drop a ball at the spot from which he's just played his second stroke and play again from there;
(ii) drop a ball behind the hazard, anywhere on the dotted line, and play from there; or
(iii) play another ball from the tee.

b Ball Lost or Unplayable Outside Hazard or Out of Bounds

If a ball played from within a *water hazard* is lost or declared unplayable outside the *hazard* or is *out of bounds*, the player, after taking **a penalty of one stroke** under Rule 27-1 or 28a, may:

(i) play a ball as nearly as possible at the spot in the *hazard* from which the original ball was last played (see Rule 20-5); or

(ii) proceed under Rule 26-1b, or if applicable Rule 26-1c, **adding the additional penalty of one stroke** prescribed by the Rule and using as the reference point the point where the original ball last crossed the margin of the *hazard* before it came to rest in the *hazard*; or

(iii) **add an additional penalty of one stroke** and play a ball as nearly as possible at the spot from which the last *stroke* from outside the *hazard* was played (see Rule 20-5).

Darren Clarke attempts to play his ball which lies in a lateral water hazard. Lateral water hazards should be defined by red stakes or lines.

Note 1: When proceeding under Rule 26-2b, the player is not required to drop a ball under Rule 27-1 or 28a. If he does drop a ball, he is not required to play it. He may alternatively proceed under Clause (ii) or (iii).

Note 2: If a ball played from within a *water hazard* is declared unplayable outside the *hazard*, nothing in Rule 26-2b precludes the player from proceeding under Rule 28b or c.

PENALTY FOR BREACH OF RULE: *Match play — Loss of hole; Stroke play — Two strokes.*

RULE 26 INCIDENT

Standing on Carnoustie's 18th tee, the 72nd hole of the 1999 British Open, Jean Van de Velde needed only a double bogey to become the first Frenchman to win the championship since 1907.

Minutes later, with his navy blue trousers rolled to his knees, he was standing in the Barry Burn contemplating his fate and his options under Rule 26.

Having played a driver from the tee, the Frenchman's ball had finished well right but safely on a peninsula created by a bend in the burn. Instead of laying up with his second, Van de Velde attempted to play a 2-iron to the distant green. His shot was a bit wayward and it ricocheted off a grandstand railing, a stone wall and finally settled behind the second crossing of the burn in heavy rough.

Attempting to chop his ball out of the rough and over the burn, he instead chunked it badly and the ball finished in the shallow water of the burn. As the stream runs perpendicular to the line of play, it was marked with a yellow line indicating a water hazard — not a lateral water hazard.

As such, Van de Velde's options were three. He could play the ball without penalty as it lay. For a one-stroke penalty, he could play again from where he last played, or he could drop behind the hazard keeping the point at which his ball last crossed the margin of the water hazard directly between the hole and the spot on which the ball would be dropped, with no limit to how far behind the hazard he might want to go.

Three in the water, and needing a six to win the British Open, the Frenchman contemplated playing out in order to avoid the penalty stroke. To make such an assessment, he decided to go into the water to see what the shot required. Having removed his shoes and socks, Van de Velde rolled up his trouser legs and lowered himself down the stone wall into the shallow water.

Van de Velde was left standing alone in the dark water, wedge in hand, assessing his ability to play the submerged ball out of the hazard. After several minutes, discretion became the better part of valor and Van de Velde chose option B under Rule 26-1. He dropped a ball behind the hazard on the stipulated line, suffered a penalty stroke and played his fifth shot to the right greenside bunker. His up-and-down from the bunker resulted in a score of seven and a playoff between Paul Lawrie, Justin Leonard and Van de Velde, which Lawrie went on to win.

RULE 27

BALL LOST OR OUT OF BOUNDS; PROVISIONAL BALL

DEFINITIONS

See **incident** involving the Definition of "Lost Ball" on page 115

A ball is "*lost*" if:

a. It is not found or identified as his by the player within five minutes after the player's *side* or his or their *caddies* have begun to search for it; or

b. The player has put another ball into play under the *Rules*, even though he may not have searched for the original ball; or

c. The player has played any stroke with a *provisional ball* from the place where the original ball is likely to be or from a point nearer the *hole* than that place, whereupon the *provisional ball* becomes the *ball in play*.

Time spent in playing a *wrong ball* is not counted in the five-minute period allowed for search.

"*Out of bounds*" is beyond the boundaries of the *course* or any part of the *course* so marked by the *Committee*.

When *out of bounds* is defined by reference to stakes or a fence, or as being beyond stakes or a fence, the *out of bounds* line is determined by the nearest inside points of the stakes or fence posts at ground level excluding angled supports.

Objects defining *out of bounds* such as walls, fences, stakes and railings, are not *obstructions* and are deemed to be fixed.

When *out of bounds* is defined by a line on the ground, the line itself is *out of bounds*.

The out of bounds line extends vertically upwards and downwards.

A ball is *out of bounds* when all of it lies *out of bounds*.

A player may stand *out of bounds* to play a ball lying within bounds.

A "*provisional ball*" is a ball played under Rule 27-2 for a ball which may be *lost* outside a *water hazard* or may be *out of bounds*.

PLAYERS UNABLE TO IDENTIFY THEIR BALLS

My ball is a number 3 with black writing.

So is mine. Unless we can identify which is which, both balls are 'lost'.

27-1 BALL LOST OR OUT OF BOUNDS

If a ball is *lost* or is *out of bounds*, the player shall play a ball, **under penalty of one stroke**, as nearly as possible at the spot from which the original ball was last played (see Rule 20-5).

Exceptions:

1. If there is reasonable evidence that the original ball is *lost* in a *water hazard*, the player shall proceed in accordance with Rule 26-1.
2. If there is reasonable evidence that the original ball is *lost* in an immovable *obstruction* (Rule 24-2c) or an *abnormal ground condition* (Rule 25-1c) the player may proceed under the applicable *Rule*.

PENALTY FOR BREACH OF RULE 27-1: *Match play — Loss of hole; Stroke play — Two strokes.*

27-2 PROVISIONAL BALL

a Procedure

If a ball may be *lost* outside a *water hazard* or may be *out of bounds*, to save time the player may play another ball provisionally in accordance with Rule 27-1. The player shall inform his opponent in match play or his *marker* or a *fellow-competitor* in stroke play that he intends to play a *provisional ball*, and he shall play it before he or his *partner* goes forward to search for the original ball.

If he fails to do so and plays another ball, such ball is not a *provisional ball* and becomes the *ball in play* **under penalty of stroke and distance** (Rule 27-1); the original ball is deemed to be *lost*.

(Order of play from *teeing ground* — see Rule 10-3.)

PROVISIONAL BALL BECOMES BALL IN PLAY

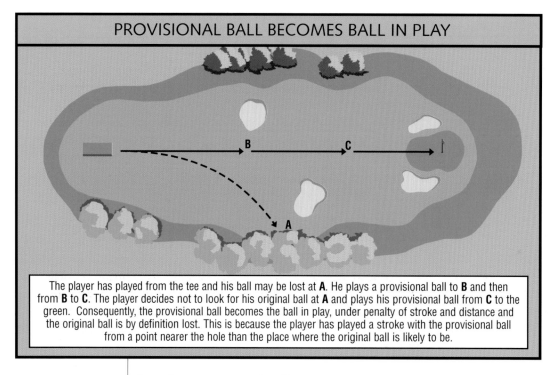

The player has played from the tee and his ball may be lost at **A**. He plays a provisional ball to **B** and then from **B** to **C**. The player decides not to look for his original ball at **A** and plays his provisional ball from **C** to the green. Consequently, the provisional ball becomes the ball in play, under penalty of stroke and distance and the original ball is by definition lost. This is because the player has played a stroke with the provisional ball from a point nearer the hole than the place where the original ball is likely to be.

b When Provisional Ball Becomes Ball in Play

The player may play a *provisional ball* until he reaches the place where the original ball is likely to be. If he plays a *stroke* with the *provisional ball* from the place where the original ball is likely to be or from a point nearer

PROVISIONAL BALL PLAYED: ORIGINAL BALL FOUND UNPLAYABLE

A player plays a provisional ball as his ball may be lost. The original ball is found within five minutes and before the provisional ball has become the ball in play, but the ball is unplayable. The player must abandon the provisional ball and proceed with the original ball.

the *hole* than that place, the original ball is deemed to be *lost* and the *provisional ball* becomes the *ball in play* **under penalty of stroke and distance** (Rule 27-1).

If the original ball is *lost* outside a *water hazard* or is *out of bounds*, the *provisional ball* becomes the *ball in play*, **under penalty of stroke and distance** (Rule 27-1).

If there is reasonable evidence that the original ball is *lost* in a *water hazard*, the player shall proceed in accordance with Rule 26-1.

Exception: If there is reasonable evidence that the original ball is *lost* in an immovable *obstruction* (Rule 24-2c) or an *abnormal ground condition* (Rule 25-1c), the player may proceed under the applicable Rule.

c When Provisional Ball to be Abandoned

If the original ball is neither *lost* nor *out of bounds*, the player shall abandon the *provisional ball* and continue play with the original ball. If he fails to do so, any further *strokes* played with the *provisional ball* shall constitute playing a *wrong ball* and the provisions of Rule 15 shall apply.

Note: *Strokes* taken and *penalty strokes* incurred solely in playing a *provisional ball* subsequently abandoned under Rule 27-2c shall be disregarded.

RULE 27 INCIDENT

During the third round of the 1998 British Open at Royal Birkdale, Mark O'Meara's second shot drifted too far to the right into knee high grass and scrub trees at the 480-yard 6th hole and put into motion a series of events that led to a clarification within the Rules of Golf.

By the time O'Meara and his caddie reached the area where they thought his ball had landed, a number of spectators were already engaged in searching for it. The Rules observer with the group was Reed Mackenzie, vice president of the USGA and chairman of its Rules of Golf Committee, who started the clock for the five-minute search period when O'Meara and his caddie reached the area.

Several balls were found, but none were O'Meara's. To everyone in the immediate vicinity, he announced the type of ball he was using and stated that it was embossed with his logo.

After searching for approximately four minutes, O'Meara suspected that his ball was lost. He left the search area, took another ball from his caddie, and started back down the fairway to play again from where his original ball had been played.

About 30 seconds later, a spectator announced, "Here it is. I have it." Someone called to O'Meara, who apparently did not hear and continued walking. An official went to where the spectator had found the ball and saw it was the type O'Meara was using and did have his logo on it.

By this time, it was nearing the end of the five-minute search period permitted under the Rules, and it was clear that O'Meara would not be able to get back to the ball in order to identify it within the five-minute period. The Definition of "Lost Ball" states that a ball is lost if it is not "found or identified" within five minutes. If the definition said, "found and identified," the procedure would have been clear. A radio call was made for a roving Rules official to make a decision.

Senior Rules Director for the PGA Tour in the U.S., Mike Shea, was working the area as an invited official and took the call. As the Rules Secretary for the Royal and Ancient Golf Club of St Andrews, David Rickman was also on hand. Shea arrived first and brought O'Meara in a cart back up the fairway where a discussion took place.

After their discussion, Shea took O'Meara back down the fairway where they met Rickman who was advised that the ball had been found, but not identified by the player, within the five-minute time limit. Considering the facts, Rickman determined that the ball had been found within the five-minute period, that O'Meara was entitled to identify it outside the stipulated time period and, if it was his ball, he was entitled to play it. Everyone returned to the area where the ball had been found.

However, during the search, the search area had been trampled and a misguided spectator, who believed the ball had been abandoned, had lifted it. When O'Meara and Rickman went to the spot, the ball was not there but the spectator was close by and returned the ball to O'Meara who identified it as his. Although the spectator said he knew "exactly" where the ball had been before he lifted it that turned out to be only an approximation.

Under Rules 18-1 and 20-3c, O'Meara was required to drop as nearly as possible to the spot where the ball had been before being lifted by the spectator. When O'Meara dropped the ball, it rolled more than two club-lengths from the spot where it struck a part of the course thus requiring a re-drop. Upon re-dropping, the ball rolled nearer to the hole and O'Meara, therefore, placed it on the spot where it first struck a part of the course when re-dropped. He then played his shot and continued the round, winning the championship the following day.

The ambiguity of the Definition of "Lost Ball," in this particular situation, necessitated the addition of Decision 27/5.5. The new decision simply clarifies that if a ball is found within five minutes, the player is allowed enough time to reach the area and identify it even though the identification takes place after the five-minute search period has elapsed.

RULE  | **BALL UNPLAYABLE**

The player may declare his ball unplayable at any place on the *course* except when the ball is in a *water hazard*. The player is the sole judge as to whether his ball is unplayable.

If the player deems his ball to be unplayable, he shall, **under penalty of one stroke:**

a. Play a ball as nearly as possible at the spot from which the original ball was last played (see Rule 20-5); or

BALL UNPLAYABLE IN BUNKER: PLAYER'S OPTIONS

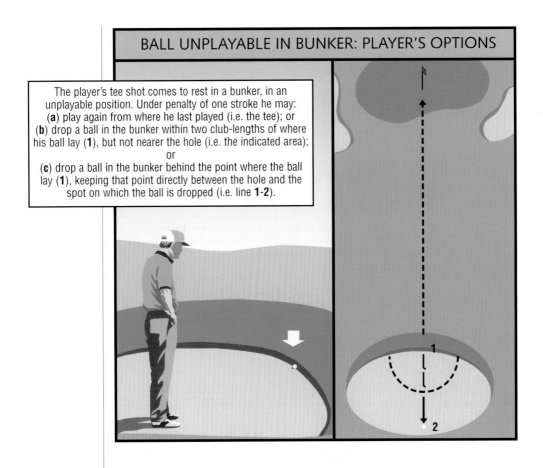

The player's tee shot comes to rest in a bunker, in an unplayable position. Under penalty of one stroke he may:
(**a**) play again from where he last played (i.e. the tee); or
(**b**) drop a ball in the bunker within two club-lengths of where his ball lay (**1**), but not nearer the hole (i.e. the indicated area); or
(**c**) drop a ball in the bunker behind the point where the ball lay (**1**), keeping that point directly between the hole and the spot on which the ball is dropped (i.e. line **1-2**).

BALL UNPLAYABLE IN BUSH: PLACE FOR DROPPING

My ball was in the bush. I've declared it unplayable, and I'm going to invoke option **b** and drop the ball within two club-lengths of where it lay.

That's O.K. But remember the ball when dropped must strike a part of the course within two club-lengths of where it lay.

b. Drop a ball within two club-lengths of the spot where the ball lay, but not nearer the *hole*; or

c. Drop a ball behind the point where the ball lay, keeping that point directly between the *hole* and the spot on which the ball is dropped, with no limit to how far behind that point the ball may be dropped.

If the unplayable ball is in a *bunker*, the player may proceed under Clause a, b or c. If he elects to proceed under Clause b or c, a ball must be dropped in the *bunker*.

The ball may be cleaned when lifted under this Rule.

PENALTY FOR BREACH OF RULE: *Match play — Loss of hole; Stroke play — Two strokes.*

See **incident** involving Rule 28 below

RULE 28 INCIDENT

A ball may be declared unplayable anywhere upon the course except in a water hazard. However, whether a ball lies in a bunker can have an important impact upon the player's options, as Corey Pavin discovered at the 1992 U.S. Open at Pebble Beach.

While it is a question of fact as to where a ball actually lies upon the course, it sometimes takes close inspection to be certain. At the 11th hole, Pavin's ball found its way under the grassy lip of a fairway bunker. At such a position it was not readily evident whether it was in the bunker or through the green.

The definition of a bunker excludes the grass-covered ground bordering or within the hazard. The margin of the bunker extends vertically downwards but not upward, and a ball is in a bunker when it lies in or any part of it touches the bunker.

By asking for a ruling, Pavin wanted to determine where he was permitted to drop his ball under the provisions of Rule 28. If his ball were not in the bunker, he would be permitted to drop outside the bunker under penalty of one stroke. If his ball were in the bunker, his only dropping option would be within the bunker.

After close examination, it was ruled that the ball was in the bunker. Pavin declared it unplayable and dropped in the hazard, keeping the point where the ball lay directly between the hole and the spot on which the ball was dropped. He incurred one penalty stroke.

RULE 29 THREESOMES AND FOURSOMES

DEFINITIONS

Threesome: A match in which one plays against two, and each *side* plays one ball.

Foursome: A match in which two play against two, and each *side* plays one ball.

29-1 GENERAL

See **incident** involving Rule 29 on page 121

In a *threesome* or a *foursome*, during any *stipulated round* the *partners* shall play alternately from the *teeing grounds* and alternately during the play of each hole. *Penalty strokes* do not affect the order of play.

FOURSOMES: ORDER OF PLAY WHEN PARTNER DRIVES OUT OF BOUNDS

That's miles out of bounds. What happens now in a mixed foursome?

Your partner must play your side's third shot from the men's tee because that's where the last shot was played from.

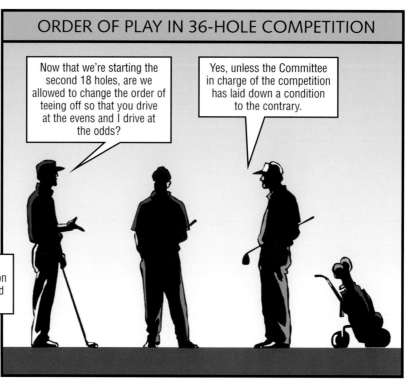

29-2 MATCH PLAY

If a player plays when his partner should have played, his *side* shall
lose the hole.

29-3 STROKE PLAY

If the *partners* play a *stroke* or *strokes* in incorrect order, such *stroke* or
strokes shall be cancelled and **the *side* shall incur a penalty of two strokes**.
The *side* shall correct the error by playing a ball in correct order as nearly as
possible at the spot from which it first played in incorrect order (see
Rule 20-5). If the *side* plays a *stroke* from the next *teeing ground* without
first correcting the error or, in the case of the last hole of the round, leaves
the *putting green* without declaring its intention to correct the error, **the
side shall be disqualified**.

RULE 29 INCIDENT

The practice putting green at the Old Course in St Andrews lies just off
the course and only a few steps from the 1st tee. Paired together on the
second day for the morning foursomes of the 1975 Walker Cup Match,
the U.S. side of veteran William C. Campbell and newcomer John
Grace reported to the tee a little ahead of time. They had already decided that Grace would drive at the odd numbered holes, so Campbell
decided to use the extra time before the match began to walk to the
practice green and hit a few putts.

As the visiting team, Campbell and Grace had the honor. The wind
was blowing from the west off St Andrews Bay, which carried the
announcement of the match's beginning beyond Campbell's earshot.

As the breeze momentarily died, Campbell heard "the click" of
Grace's drive just before striking a practice putt, and he was unable to
interrupt his stroke. He had practiced during the play of the hole.
Instantly and instinctively recognizing his violation, Campbell walked
onto the fairway and reported to the referee that the U.S. had lost the
first hole. [Rule 7-2 and Rule 29.]

The referee for the match, John Pasquill from the Royal and
Ancient Golf Club, accepted Campbell's report but made no immediate
announcement to the other players. Because play of the hole had ended
with the Rules violation and the loss of hole, Campbell was free to play
his side's second from where Grace's good drive lay to the green, as
simply more practice.

Walking across the Swilken Burn, Campbell told Grace what had
taken place. "He was incredulous, to say the least," Campbell recalls.

The fact that the practice green was off the course, beyond the out
of bounds markers, gave Grace reason to believe they might have a
chance on appeal, though there is no such distinction within the Rules.

Campbell reported to Pasquill that his partner wished to protest
the ruling and appeal to the Committee. In a neutral voice, Pasquill
appropriately replied, "On the golf course, I am the Committee." The
Americans lost the first hole and eventually lost the match to Mark
James and Richard Eyles.

RULE 30

THREE-BALL, BEST-BALL AND FOUR-BALL MATCH PLAY

DEFINITIONS

Three-Ball: A match play competition in which three play against one another, each playing his own ball. Each player is playing two distinct *matches*.

Best-Ball: A match in which one plays against the better ball of two or the best ball of three players.

Four-Ball: A match in which two play their better ball against the better ball of two other players.

30-1 RULES OF GOLF APPLY

The Rules of Golf, so far as they are not at variance with the following special Rules, shall apply to three-ball, best-ball and four-ball *matches*.

30-2 THREE-BALL MATCH PLAY
a Ball at Rest Moved by an Opponent

Except as otherwise provided in the *Rules*, if the player's ball is touched or *moved* by an opponent, his *caddie* or *equipment* other than during search, Rule 18-3b applies. **That opponent shall incur a *penalty stroke* in his match with the player**, but not in his match with the other opponent.

b Ball Deflected or Stopped by an Opponent Accidentally

If a player's ball is accidentally deflected or stopped by an opponent, his *caddie* or *equipment*, no penalty shall be incurred. In his match with that

BREACH OF RULE BY ONE PARTNER IN MATCH PLAY

I'll just remove this twig.

I'm afraid you're disqualified from the hole for removing a loose impediment from the bunker.
Fortunately, although I'm in the same bunker I'm not penalized because your breach of Rule 13-4 did not assist my play.

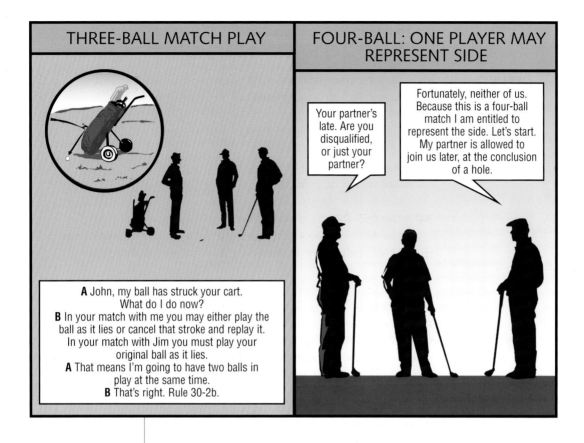

THREE-BALL MATCH PLAY

A John, my ball has struck your cart. What do I do now?
B In your match with me you may either play the ball as it lies or cancel that stroke and replay it. In your match with Jim you must play your original ball as it lies.
A That means I'm going to have two balls in play at the same time.
B That's right. Rule 30-2b.

FOUR-BALL: ONE PLAYER MAY REPRESENT SIDE

Your partner's late. Are you disqualified, or just your partner?

Fortunately, neither of us. Because this is a four-ball match I am entitled to represent the side. Let's start. My partner is allowed to join us later, at the conclusion of a hole.

opponent the player may play the ball as it lies or, before another *stroke* is played by either *side*, he may cancel the *stroke* and play a ball without penalty as nearly as possible at the spot from which the original ball was last played (see Rule 20-5). In his match with the other opponent, the ball shall be played as it lies.

Exception: Ball striking person attending *flagstick* — see Rule 17-3b.

(Ball purposely deflected or stopped by an opponent — see Rule 1-2.)

30-3 BEST-BALL AND FOUR-BALL MATCH PLAY
a Representation of Side
A *side* may be represented by one *partner* for all or any part of a match; all *partners* need not be present. An absent *partner* may join a match between holes, but not during play of a hole.

b Maximum of Fourteen Clubs
The *side* shall be penalized for a breach of Rule 4-4 by any *partner*.

c Order of Play
Balls belonging to the same *side* may be played in the order the *side* considers best.

d Wrong Ball
If a player plays a *stroke* with a *wrong ball* except in a *hazard*, **he shall be disqualified for that hole**, but his *partner* incurs no penalty even if the *wrong*

123

ball belongs to him. If the *wrong ball* belongs to another player, its owner shall place a ball on the spot from which the *wrong ball* was first played.

e Disqualification of Side

(i)   **A side shall be disqualified** for a breach of any of the following by any *partner*:

Rule 1-3	Agreement to Waive Rules.
Rule 4-1 or -2	Clubs.
Rule 5-1 or -2	The Ball.
Rule 6-2a	Handicap (playing off higher handicap).
Rule 6-4	*Caddie*.
Rule 6-7	Undue Delay; Slow Play (repeated offense).
Rule 14-3	Artificial Devices and Unusual *Equipment*.

(ii)   **A *side* shall be disqualified** for a breach of any of the following by all *partners*:

Rule 6-3	Time of Starting and Groups.
Rule 6-8	Discontinuance of Play.

f Effects of Other Penalties

If a player's breach of a *Rule* assists his *partner's* play or adversely affects an opponent's play, **the *partner* incurs the applicable penalty in addition to any penalty incurred by the player.**

In all other cases where a player incurs a penalty for breach of a *Rule*, the penalty shall not apply to his *partner*. Where the penalty is stated to be loss of hole, the effect shall be to disqualify the player for that hole.

g Another Form of Match Played Concurrently

In a best-ball or four-ball match when another form of match is played concurrently, the above special Rules shall apply.

RULE 31 FOUR-BALL STROKE PLAY

In four-ball stroke play two *competitors* play as *partners*, each playing his own ball. The lower score of the *partners* is the score for the hole. If one *partner* fails to complete the play of a hole, there is no penalty.

31-1 RULES OF GOLF APPLY

The Rules of Golf, so far as they are not at variance with the following special Rules, shall apply to four-ball stroke play.

31-2 REPRESENTATION OF SIDE

A *side* may be represented by either *partner* for all or any part of a *stipulated round*; both *partners* need not be present. An absent *competitor* may join his *partner* between holes, but not during play of a hole.

FOUR BALL STROKE PLAY

Date _3RD APRIL 1996_

Competition _SPRING OPEN FOUR-BALL_

PLAYER A _J. SUTHERLAND_   Handicap _16_   Strokes _12_

PLAYER B _W. B. TAYLOR_   Handicap _12_   Strokes _9_

Hole	Length Yards	Par	Stroke Index	Gross Score A	Gross Score B	Net Score A	Net Score B	Won X Lost – Half O	Mar. Score	Hole	Length Yards	Par	Stroke Index	Gross Score A	Gross Score B	Net Score A	Net Score B	Won X Lost – Half O	Mar. Score
1	437	4	4		4		3			10	425	4	3		5		4		
2	320	4	14		4		4			11	141	3	17	3		3			
3	162	3	18		4		4			12	476	5	9	6		5			
4	504	5	7	6		5				13	211	3	11		4		4		
5	181	3	16	4		4				14	437	4	5		5		4		
6	443	4	2		5	4				15	460	4	1		5		4		
7	390	4	8		5	4				16	176	3	15	4		4			
8	346	4	12	5		4				17	340	4	13		4		4		
9	340	4	10	4		3				18	435	4	6	6		5			
Out	3123	35				35				In	3101	34				37			
										Out	3123	35				35			
										T'tl	6224	69				72			

Player's Signature _J. Sutherland_

Marker's Signature _R. J. Parker_

Handicap					
Net Score					

PARTNER'S SCORES TO BE INDIVIDUALLY IDENTIFIED

1. The lower score of the partners is the score for the hole (Rule 31)

2. Only one of the partners need be responsible for complying with Rule 6-6b i.e. recording scores, checking scores, countersigning and returning the card (Rule 31-4).

3. The competitor is solely responsible for the correctness of the gross score recorded. Although there is no objection to the competitor (or his marker) entering the net score, it is the Committee's responsibility to record the better ball score for each hole, to add up the scores and to apply the handicaps recorded on the card (Rule 33-5). Thus there is no penalty for an error by the competitor (or his marker) for recording an incorrect net score.

4. Scores of the two partners must be kept in separate columns otherwise it is impossible for the Committee to apply the correct handicap. If the scores of both partners, having different handicaps, are recorded in the same column, the Committee has no alternative but to disqualify both partners (Rules 31-7 and 6-6 apply).

5. The Committee is responsible for laying down the conditions under which a competition is to be played (Rule 33-1), including the method of handicapping. In the above illustration the Committee laid down that ¾ handicaps would apply.

31-3 MAXIMUM OF FOURTEEN CLUBS
The *side* **shall be penalized** for a breach of Rule 4-4 by either *partner*.

31-4 SCORING
The *marker* is required to record for each hole only the gross score of whichever *partner's* score is to count. The gross scores to count must be individually identifiable; otherwise **the *side* shall be disqualified**. Only one of the *partners* need be responsible for complying with Rule 6-6b.
(Wrong score — see Rule 31-7a.)

31-5 ORDER OF PLAY
Balls belonging to the same *side* may be played in the order the *side* considers best.

31-6 WRONG BALL
If a *competitor* plays a *stroke* or *strokes* with a *wrong ball* except in a *hazard*, **he shall add two *penalty strokes* to his score for the hole** and shall then play the correct ball. His *partner* incurs no penalty even if the *wrong ball* belongs to him.

If the wrong ball belongs to another *competitor*, its owner shall place a ball on the spot from which the *wrong ball* was first played.

31-7 DISQUALIFICATION PENALTIES
a Breach by One Partner
A *side* **shall be disqualified from the competition** for a breach of any of the following by either *partner*:

Rule 1-3	Agreement to Waive Rules.
Rule 3-4	Refusal to Comply with Rule.
Rule 4-1 or -2	Clubs.
Rule 5-1 or -2	The Ball.
Rule 6-2b	Handicap (playing off higher handicap; failure to record handicap).
Rule 6-4	*Caddie*.
Rule 6-6b	Signing and Returning Card.
Rule 6-6d	Wrong Score for Hole, i.e. when the recorded score of the *partner* whose score is to count is lower the actually taken. If the recorded score of the *partner* whose score is to count is higher than actually taken, it must stand as returned.
Rule 6-7	Undue Delay; Slow Play (repeated offence).
Rule 7-1	Practice Before or Between Rounds.
Rule 14-3	Artificial Devices and Unusual *Equipment*.
Rule 31-4	Gross Scores to Count Not Individually Identifiable.

b Breach by Both Partners
A *side* shall be disqualified:
(i) for a breach by both *partners* of Rule 6-3 (Time of Starting and Groups) or Rule 6-8 (Discontinuance of Play), or
(ii) if, at the same hole, each *partner* is in breach of a *Rule* the penalty for which is disqualification from the competition or for a hole.

c For the Hole Only

In all other cases where a breach of a *Rule* would entail disqualification, **the competitor shall be disqualified only for the hole at which the breach occurred**.

31-8 EFFECT OF OTHER PENALTIES

If a *competitor's* breach of a *Rule* assists his *partner's* play, **the *partner* incurs the applicable penalty in addition to any penalty incurred by the *competitor***.

In all other cases where a *competitor* incurs a penalty for breach of a *Rule*, the penalty shall not apply to his *partner*.

RULE 32

BOGEY, PAR AND STABLEFORD COMPETITIONS

32-1 CONDITIONS

Bogey, par and Stableford competitions are forms of stroke competition in which play is against a fixed score at each hole. The Rules for stroke play, so far as they are not at variance with the following special Rules, apply.

a Bogey and Par Competitions

The reckoning for bogey and par competitions is made as in match play. Any hole for which a *competitor* makes no return shall be regarded as a loss. The winner is the *competitor* who is most successful in the aggregate of holes.

The *marker* is responsible for marking only the gross number of *strokes* for each hole where the *competitor* makes a net score equal to or less than the fixed score.

Note 1: Maximum of 14 Clubs — Penalties as in match play — see Rule 4-4.
Note 2: Undue Delay; Slow Play (Rule 6-7) — The player's score shall be adjusted by deducting one hole from the overall result.

b Stableford Competitions

The reckoning in Stableford competitions is made by points awarded in relation to a fixed score at each hole as follows:

Hole Played in	Points
More than one over fixed score or no score returned	0
One over fixed score	1
Fixed Score	2
One under fixed score	3
Two under fixed score	4
Three under fixed score	5
Four under fixed score	6

The winner is the *competitor* who scores the highest number of points.

The *marker* shall be responsible for marking only the gross number of *strokes* at each hole where the *competitor's* net score earns one or more points.

Note 1: Maximum of 14 Clubs (Rule 4-4) — Penalties applied as follows: From total points scored for the round, deduction of two points for each hole at which any breach occurred; maximum deduction per round: four points.

Note 2: Undue Delay; Slow Play (Rule 6-7) — The player's score shall be adjusted by deducting two points from the points total scored for the round.

32-2 DISQUALIFICATION PENALTIES
a From the Competition
A *competitor* **shall be disqualified** from the competition for a breach of any of the following:

Rule 1-3	Agreement to Waive Rules.
Rule 3-4	Refusal to Comply with Rule.
Rule 4-1 or -2	Clubs.
Rule 5-1 or -2	The Ball.
Rule 6-2b	Handicap (playing off higher handicap; failure to record handicap).
Rule 6-3	Time of Starting and Groups.
Rule 6-4	*Caddie*.
Rule 6-6b	Signing and Returning Card.
Rule 6-6d	Wrong Score for Hole, except that no penalty shall be incurred when a breach of this Rule does not affect the result of the hole.
Rule 6-7	Undue Delay; Slow Play (repeated offence).
Rule 6-8	Discontinuance of Play.
Rule 7-1	Practice Before or Between Rounds.
Rule 14-3	Artificial Devices and Unusual *Equipment*.

b For a Hole
In all other cases where a breach of a *Rule* would entail disqualification, **the *competitor* shall be disqualified only for the hole at which the breach occurred**.

RULE

THE COMMITTEE

See **incident** involving Rule 33-1 on page 131

33-1 CONDITIONS; WAIVING RULE
The *Committee* shall lay down the conditions under which a competition is to be played.

The *Committee* has no power to waive a Rule of Golf.

Certain special rules governing stroke play are so substantially different from those governing match play that combining the two forms of play is not practicable and is not permitted. The results of *matches* played and the scores returned in these circumstances shall not be accepted.

In stroke play the *Committee* may limit a *referee's* duties.

33-2 THE COURSE
a Defining Bounds and Margins
The *Committee* shall define accurately:

(i)   the *course* and *out of bounds*,
(ii)   the margins of *water hazards* and *lateral water hazards*,
(iii) *ground under repair*, and
(iv)   *obstructions* and integral parts of the *course*.

b New Holes

New *holes* should be made on the day on which a stroke competition begins and at such other times as the *Committee* considers necessary, provided all *competitors* in a single round play with each *hole* cut in the same position.
Exception: When it is impossible for a damaged *hole* to be repaired so that it conforms with the Definition, the *Committee* may make a new *hole* in a nearby similar position.
Note: Where a single round is to be played on more than one day, the *Committee* may provide in the conditions of a competition that the *holes* and *teeing grounds* may be differently situated on each day of the competition, provided that, on any one day, all *competitors* play with each *hole* and each *teeing ground* in the same position.

c Practice Ground

Where there is no practice ground available outside the area of a competition *course*, the *Committee* should lay down the area on which players may practice on any day of a competition, if it is practicable to do so. On any day of a stroke competition, the *Committee* should not normally permit practice on or to a *putting green* or from a *hazard* of the competition *course*.

d Course Unplayable

If the *Committee* or its authorized representative considers that for any reason the *course* is not in a playable condition or that there are circumstances which render the proper playing of the game impossible,

If the course is not in a playable condition, the Committee may have to temporarily suspend play. In stroke play only, if further play becomes impossible, the Committee may have to declare play null and void.

it may, in match play or stroke play, order a temporary suspension of play or, in stroke play, declare play null and void and cancel all scores for the round in question. When a round is cancelled, all penalties incurred in that round are cancelled.

(Procedure in discontinuing play — see Rule 6-8.)

33-3 TIMES OF STARTING AND GROUPS

The *Committee* shall lay down the times of starting and, in stroke play, arrange the groups in which *competitors* shall play.

When a match play competition is played over an extended period, the *Committee* shall lay down the limit of time within which each round shall be completed. When players are allowed to arrange the date of their match within these limits, the *Committee* should announce that the match must be played at a stated time on the last day of the period unless the players agree to a prior date.

33-4 HANDICAP STROKE TABLE

The *Committee* shall publish a table indicating the order of holes at which handicap strokes are to be given or received.

33-5 SCORE CARD

In stroke play, the *Committee* shall issue for each *competitor* a score card containing the date and the *competitor's* name or, in foursome or four-ball stroke play, the *competitors'* names.

In stroke play, the *Committee* is responsible for the addition of scores and application of the handicap recorded on the card.

In four-ball stroke play, the *Committee* is responsible for recording the better-ball score for each hole and in the process applying the handicaps recorded on the card, and adding the better-ball scores.

In bogey, par and Stableford competitions, the *Committee* is responsible for applying the handicap recorded on the card and determining the result of each hole and the overall result or points total.

33-6 DECISION OF TIES

The *Committee* shall announce the manner, day and time for the decision of a halved match or of a tie, whether played on level terms or under handicap.

A halved match shall not be decided by stroke play. A tie in stroke play shall not be decided by a match.

33-7 DISQUALIFICATION PENALTY; COMMITTEE DISCRETION

A penalty of disqualification may in exceptional individual cases be waived, modified or imposed if the *Committee* considers such action warranted.

Any penalty less than disqualification shall not be waived or modified.

33-8 LOCAL RULES
a Policy

The *Committee* may make and publish Local Rules for local abnormal conditions if they are consistent with the policy set forth in Appendix I.

b Waiving Penalty

A Rule of Golf shall not be waived by a Local Rule. However, if a *Committee* considers that local abnormal conditions interfere with the proper playing of the game to the extent that it is necessary to make a Local Rule which modifies the Rules of Golf, the Local Rule must be authorized by the USGA.

RULE 33 INCIDENT

Prior to the opening round of the second U.S. Open, the USGA's first president, Theodore Havemeyer, made what is arguably the most important ruling in the championship's long history.

The championship was held during July 1896 at Shinnecock Hills Golf Club on Long Island and was precluded by a situation which led Havemeyer to establish the Committee's unequivocal authority, as stated in Rule 33, to lay down the conditions under which a competition is to be played.

Gathering before the opening round, a group of competitors, comprised of proficient or professional players mostly from Scotland, England, and private clubs in New York, New England and Chicago, objected to John Shippen being accepted into the competitive field. Shippen's mother was a Shinnecock Indian and his father was a black, Presbyterian minister on the nearby Shinnecock Indian Reservation.

The objectors threatened that, if forced to play with Shippen, they would withdraw from the competition, thereby leaving a weaker field and a dubious U.S. Open champion. At this early point in the game's history in the U.S., those less knowledgeable of the game generally deferred to those proficient at playing it to help mold competitive policies and procedures. Such a dilemma extended to golf in the 1890s. Fortunately, Havemeyer provided insight and direction on his side of the equation.

He met with the objectors and made the USGA's argument succinctly: An open competition was to be held; in order to be an open competition, applications had been accepted from all qualified individuals; to limit the field on any basis would invalidate the open nature of the competition and, in turn, the identification of the national open champion.

Havemeyer emphasized that it was the objectors' unquestioned right to decide whether or not they would compete. However, as far as the national championship was concerned, if Shippen chose to play and he were the only competitor in the field, Shippen would be the national champion.

Feeling the intransigence of Havemeyer's argument and his irrefutable logic, those objecting reversed themselves and chose to compete. James Foulis, a Scottish professional playing out of the Chicago Golf Club was the champion with a score of 152. Shippen tied for fifth.

RULE **34** DISPUTES AND DECISIONS

34-1 CLAIMS AND PENALTIES
a Match Play

In match play if a claim is lodged with the *Committee* under Rule 2-5, a decision should be given as soon as possible so that the state of the match may, if necessary, be adjusted.

If a claim is not made within the time limit provided by Rule 2-5, it shall not be considered unless it is based on facts previously unknown to the player making the claim and the player making the claim had been given wrong information (Rules 6-2a and 9) by an opponent. In any case, no later claim shall be considered after the result of the match has been officially announced, unless the *Committee* is satisfied that the opponent knew he was giving wrong information.

There is no time limit on applying the disqualification penalty for a breach of Rule 1-3.

b Stroke Play

Except as provided below, in stroke play, no penalty shall be rescinded, modified or imposed after the competition has closed. A competition is deemed to have closed when the result has been officially announced or, in stroke play qualifying followed by match play, when the player has teed off in his first match.

Exceptions: A penalty of disqualification shall be imposed after the competition has closed if a *competitor*:

(i)   was in breach of Rule 1-3 (Agreement to Waive Rules); or
(ii)   returned a score card on which he had recorded a handicap which, before the competition closed, he knew was higher than that to which he was entitled, and this affected the number of strokes received (Rule 6-2b); or
(iii) returned a score for any hole lower than actually taken (Rule 6-6d) for any reason other than failure to include a penalty which, before the competition closed, he did not know he had incurred; or
(iv)   knew, before the competition closed, that he had been in breach of any other *Rule* for which the prescribed penalty is disqualification.

34-2 REFEREE'S DECISION

If a *referee* has been appointed by the *Committee*, his decision shall be final.

34-3 COMMITTEE'S DECISION

In the absence of a *referee*, any dispute or doubtful point on the Rules shall be referred to the *Committee*, whose decision shall be final.

If the *Committee* cannot come to a decision, it shall refer the dispute or doubtful point to the Rules of Golf Committee of the United States Golf Association, whose decision shall be final.

If the dispute or doubtful point has not been referred to the Rules of Golf Committee, the player or players have the right to refer an agreed statement through the Secretary of the Club to the Rules of Golf Committee for an opinion as to the correctness of the decision given. The reply will be sent to the Secretary of the Club or Clubs concerned.

If play is conducted other than in accordance with the Rules of Golf, the Rules of Golf Committee will not give a decision on any question.

APPENDIX I

LOCAL RULES; CONDITIONS OF THE COMPETITION

LOCAL RULES INCIDENT

Nick Faldo learned the hard way that it is always necessary to ascertain which Local Rules have been adopted for a competition and, just as importantly, which have not.

The Royal and Ancient Golf Club of St. Andrews and the PGA European Tour have for years employed in their championships a Local Rule allowing the removal of stones in bunkers by declaring the stones to be movable obstructions. Faldo was accustomed to playing under such a Local Rule.

In the autumn of 1994, however, he ran into trouble in a bunker during the third round of the Alfred Dunhill Masters in Bali. Believing erroneously that the removal of stones was sanctioned in the Bali event as it was on the European tour, Faldo employed the Local Rule during the third round.

On the following day, a competitor was almost penalized for removing a stone in a bunker. The player's confusion stemmed from the fact that Faldo had removed a stone from a bunker the previous day.

Leading the tournament by six strokes with just six holes remaining, Faldo was called off the course. Because the three-time British Open Champion and two-time Masters Champion had returned his score card for the third round and did not include two penalty strokes for his infraction, he was disqualified.

PART A: LOCAL RULES

As provided in Rule 33-8a, the *Committee* may make and publish Local Rules for local abnormal conditions if they are consistent with the policy set forth in this Appendix. In addition, detailed information regarding acceptable and prohibited Local Rules is provided in "Decisions on the Rules of Golf" under Rule 33-8.

If local abnormal conditions interfere with the proper playing of the game and the *Committee* considers it necessary to modify a Rule of Golf, authorization from the United States Golf Association must be obtained.

1 DEFINING BOUNDS AND MARGINS

Specifying means used to define *out of bounds, water hazards, lateral water hazards, ground under repair, obstructions* and integral parts of the *course* (Rule 33-2a).

2 WATER HAZARDS

a *Lateral Water Hazards.*
Clarifying the status of *water hazards* which may be *lateral water hazards* (Rule 26).

b *Provisional Ball.*
Permitting play of a *provisional ball* for a ball which may be in a *water hazard* of such character that if the original ball is not found, there is reasonable evidence that it is *lost* in the *water hazard* and it would be impracticable to determine whether the ball is in the *hazard* or to do so would unduly delay play. The ball shall be played provisionally under any of the available options under Rule 26-1 or any applicable Local Rule. In such a case, if a *provisional ball* is played and the original ball is in a *water hazard*, the player may play the original ball as it lies or continue with the *provisional ball* in play, but he may not

133

proceed under Rule 26-1 with regard to the original ball.

3 AREAS OF THE COURSE REQUIRING PRESERVATION; ENVIRONMENTALLY-SENSITIVE AREAS

Assisting preservation of the *course* by defining areas, including turf nurseries, young plantations and other parts of the *course* under cultivation, as *"ground under repair"* from which play is prohibited.

When the *Committee* is required to prohibit play from environmentally-sensitive areas which are on or adjoin the *course*, it should make a Local Rule clarifying the relief procedure.

4 TEMPORARY CONDITIONS – MUD, EXTREME WETNESS, POOR CONDITIONS AND PROTECTION OF COURSE

a Lifting an Embedded Ball, Cleaning

Temporary conditions which might interfere with the proper playing of the game, including mud and extreme wetness, warranting relief for an embedded ball anywhere *through the green* or permitting lifting, cleaning and replacing a ball anywhere *through the green* or on a closely-mown area *through the green*.

b "Preferred Lies" and "Winter Rules"

Adverse conditions, including the poor condition of the *course* or the existence of mud, are sometimes so general, particularly during winter months, that the *Committee* may decide to grant relief by temporary Local Rule either to protect the *course* or to promote fair and pleasant play. Such Local Rule shall be withdrawn as soon as the conditions warrant.

5 OBSTRUCTIONS

a General

Clarifying the status of objects which may be *obstructions* (Rule 24).

Declaring any construction to be an integral part of the *course* and, accordingly, not an *obstruction*, e.g., built-up sides of *teeing grounds*, *putting greens* and *bunkers* (Rules 24 and 33-2a).

b Stones in Bunkers

Allowing the removal of stones in *bunkers* by declaring them to be "movable *obstructions*" (Rule 24-1).

c Roads and Paths

(i) Declaring artificial surfaces and sides of roads and paths to be integral parts of the *course*, or

(ii) Providing relief of the type afforded under Rule 24-2b from roads and paths not having artificial surfaces and sides if they could unfairly affect play.

d Fixed Sprinkler Heads

Providing relief from intervention by fixed sprinkler heads on or within two club-lengths of the *putting green* when the ball lies within two club-lengths of the sprinkler head.

e Protection of Young Trees

Providing relief for the protection of young trees.

f Temporary Obstructions

Providing relief from interference by temporary *obstructions* (e.g., grandstands, television cables and equipment, etc.).

6 DROPPING ZONES (BALL DROPS)

Establishing special areas on which balls may or shall be dropped when it is not feasible or practicable to proceed exactly in conformity with Rule 24-2b or 24-2c (*Immovable Obstruction*), Rule 25-1b or 25-1c (*Abnormal Ground Conditions*), Rule 25-3 (*Wrong Putting Green*), Rule 26-1 (*Water Hazards* and *Lateral Water Hazards*) or Rule 28 (*Ball Unplayable*).

PART B: SPECIMEN LOCAL RULES

Within the policy set out in Part A of this Appendix, the *Committee* may adopt a Specimen Local Rule by referring, on a score card or notice board, to the examples given below. However, Specimen Local Rules 3a, 3b, 3c, 6a and 6b should not be printed or referred to on a score card as they are all of limited duration.

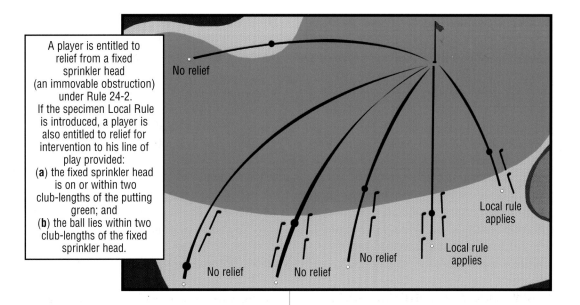

A player is entitled to relief from a fixed sprinkler head (an immovable obstruction) under Rule 24-2.
If the specimen Local Rule is introduced, a player is also entitled to relief for intervention to his line of play provided:
(**a**) the fixed sprinkler head is on or within two club-lengths of the putting green; and
(**b**) the ball lies within two club-lengths of the fixed sprinkler head.

No relief

No relief

No relief

No relief

Local rule applies

Local rule applies

1 AREAS OF THE COURSE REQUIRING PRESERVATION; ENVIRONMENTALLY-SENSITIVE AREAS

a Ground Under Repair; Play Prohibited

If the *Committee* wishes to protect any area of the *course*, it should declare it to be *ground under repair* and prohibit play from within that area. The following Local Rule is recommended:

"The _____ (defined by _____) is *ground under repair* from which play is prohibited. If a player's ball lies in the area, or if it interferes with the player's *stance* or the area of his intended swing, the player must take relief under Rule 25-1.

PENALTY FOR BREACH OF LOCAL RULE: *Match play – Loss of hole; Stroke play – Two strokes.*"

The Links course at Spanish Bay in California has areas of sand dunes which have been declared environmentally-sensitive. A player may not play from or enter these areas.

b Environmentally-Sensitive Areas

If an appropriate authority (i.e., a Government Agency or the like) prohibits entry into and/or play from an area on or adjoining the course for environmental reasons, the *Committee* should make a Local Rule clarifying the relief procedure.

The *Committee* has some discretion in terms of whether the area is defined as *ground under repair*, a *water hazard* or *out of bounds*. However, it may not simply define such an area to be a *water hazard* if it does not meet the Definition of a *"Water Hazard"* and it should attempt to preserve the character of the hole.

The following Local Rule is recommended:

"I Definition

An environmentally-sensitive area is an area so declared by an appropriate authority, entry into and/or play from which is prohibited for environmental reasons. Such an area may be defined as *ground under repair*, a *water hazard*, a *lateral water hazard* or *out of bounds* at the discretion of the *Committee* provided that, in the case of an environmentally-sensitive area which has been defined as a *water hazard* or a *lateral water hazard*, the area is, by Definition, a *water hazard*.

Note: The *Committee* may not declare an area to be environmentally-sensitive.

II Ball in Environmentally-Sensitive Area
a Ground Under Repair

If a ball is in an environmentally-sensitive area which is defined as *ground under repair*, a ball must be dropped in accordance with Rule 25-1b.

If there is reasonable evidence that a ball is *lost* within an environmentally-sensitive area which is defined as *ground under repair*, the player may take relief without penalty as prescribed in Rule 25-1c.

b Water Hazards and Lateral Water Hazards

If a ball is in or there is reasonable evidence that it is *lost* in an environmentally-sensitive area which is defined as a *water hazard* or *lateral water hazard*, the player must, **under penalty of one stroke**, proceed under Rule 26-1.

Note: If a ball dropped in accordance with Rule 26 rolls into a position where the environmentally-sensitive area interferes with the player's *stance* or the area of his intended swing, the player must take relief as provided in Clause 3 of this Local Rule.

c Out of Bounds

If a ball is in an environmentally-sensitive area which is defined as *out of bounds*, the player shall play a ball, **under penalty of one stroke**, as nearly as possible at the spot from which the original ball was last played (see Rule 20-5).

III Interference with Stance or Area of Intended Swing

Interference by an environmentally-sensitive area occurs when such a condition interferes with the player's *stance* or the area of his intended swing. If interference exists, the player must take relief as follows:

(i) **Through the Green:** If the ball lies *through the green*, the point on the *course* nearest to where the ball lies shall be determined which (a) is not nearer the *hole*, (b) avoids interference by the condition and (c) is not in a *hazard* or on a *putting green*. The player shall lift the ball and drop it without penalty within one club-length of the point thus determined on a part of the *course* that fulfils (a), (b) and (c) above.

(ii) **In a Hazard:** If the ball is in a *hazard*, the player shall lift the ball and drop it either: (a) Without penalty, in the *hazard*, as near as possible to the spot where the ball lay, but not nearer the *hole*, on a part of the *course* which provides complete relief from the condition; or (b) **Under penalty of one stroke**, outside the *hazard*, keeping the point where the ball lay directly between the *hole* and the spot on which the ball is dropped, with no limit to how far behind the *hazard* the ball may be dropped. Additionally, the player may proceed under Rule 26 or 28 if applicable.

(iii) **On the Putting Green:** If the ball lies on the *putting green*, the player shall lift the ball and place it without penalty in the nearest

position to where it lay which affords complete relief from the condition, but not nearer the *hole* or in a *hazard*.

The ball may be cleaned when so lifted under Clause 3 of this Local Rule.

Exception: A player may not obtain relief under Clause 3 of this Local Rule if (a) it is clearly unreasonable for him to play a *stroke* because of interference by anything other than a condition covered by this Local Rule or (b) interference by such a condition would occur only through use of an unnecessarily abnormal *stance*, swing or direction of play.

PENALTY FOR BREACH OF LOCAL RULE: *Match play – Loss of hole; Stroke play – Two strokes.*

Note: In case of a serious breach of this Local Rule, the *Committee* may impose a penalty of disqualification."

2 PROTECTION OF YOUNG TREES

When it is desired to prevent damage to young trees, the following Local Rule is recommended:

"Protection of young trees identified by _____ . If such a tree interferes with a player's *stance* or the area of his intended swing, the ball must be lifted, without penalty, and dropped in accordance with the procedure prescribed in Rule 24-2b (Immovable *Obstruction*). If the ball lies in a *water hazard*, the player shall lift and drop the ball in accordance with Rule 24-2b(i) except that the *nearest point of relief* must be in the *water hazard* and the ball must be dropped in the *water hazard* or the player may proceed under Rule 26. The ball may be cleaned when so lifted.

Exception: A player may not obtain relief under this Local Rule if (a) it is clearly unreasonable for him to play a *stroke* because of interference by anything other than such tree or (b) interference by such tree would occur only through use of an unnecessarily abnormal *stance*, swing or direction of play.

PENALTY FOR BREACH OF LOCAL RULE: *Match play — Loss of hole; Stroke play — Two strokes.*"

137

3 TEMPORARY CONDITIONS – MUD, EXTREME WETNESS, POOR CONDITIONS AND PROTECTION OF THE COURSE

a Relief for Embedded Ball; Cleaning Ball

Rule 25-2 provides relief without penalty for a ball embedded in its own pitch-mark in any closely-mown area *through the green*. On the *putting green*, a ball may be lifted and damage caused by the impact of a ball may be repaired (Rules 16-1b and c). When permission to take relief for an embedded ball anywhere *through the green* would be warranted, the following Local Rule is recommended:

"*Through the green*, a ball which is embedded in its own pitch-mark in the ground, other than sand, may be lifted without penalty, cleaned and dropped as near as possible to where it lay but not nearer the *hole*. The ball when dropped must first strike a part of the *course through the green*.

Exception: A player may not obtain relief under this Local Rule if it is clearly unreasonable for him to play a *stroke* because of interference by anything other than the condition covered by this Local Rule.

PENALTY FOR BREACH OF LOCAL RULE: *Match play — Loss of hole; Stroke play — Two strokes."*

Alternatively, conditions may be such that permission to lift, clean and replace the ball will suffice. In such circumstances, the following Local Rule is recommended:
"(Specify area) a ball may be lifted, cleaned and replaced without penalty.
Note: The position of the ball shall be marked before it is lifted under this Local Rule – see Rule 20-1.
PENALTY FOR BREACH OF LOCAL RULE: *Match play — Loss of hole; Stroke play — Two strokes."*

b "Preferred Lies" and "Winter Rules"

The USGA does not endorse "preferred lies" or "winter rules" and recommends that the Rules of Golf be observed uniformly. *Ground under repair* is provided for in Rule 25 and occasional local abnormal conditions which might interfere with fair play and are not widespread should be defined as *ground under repair*.

However, adverse conditions are sometimes so general throughout a *course* that the *Committee* believes "preferred lies" or "winter rules" would promote fair play or help protect the *course*. Heavy snows, spring thaws, prolonged rains or extreme heat can make fairways unsatisfactory and sometimes prevent use of heavy mowing equipment.

When a *Committee* adopts a Local Rule for "preferred lies" or "winter rules" it should be set out in detail and should be interpreted by the *Committee*, as there is no established code for "winter rules". Without a detailed Local Rule, it is meaningless for a *Committee* to post a notice merely saying "Winter Rules today."

The following Local Rule would seem appropriate for the conditions in question, but the USGA will not interpret it:
"A ball lying on a closely-mown area *through the green* may, without penalty, be moved or may be lifted, cleaned and placed within (specify area, e.g., six inches, one club-length, etc.) of where it originally lay, but not nearer the *hole* and not in a *hazard* or on a *putting green*. A player may move or place his ball once and after the ball has been so moved or placed, it is in play.
PENALTY FOR BREACH OF LOCAL RULE: *Match play – Loss of hole; Stroke play – Two strokes."*

Before a *Committee* adopts a Local Rule permitting "preferred lies" or "winter rules", the following facts should be considered:
1. Such a Local Rule conflicts with the Rules of Golf and the fundamental principle of playing the ball as it lies.
2. "Winter rules" are sometimes adopted under the guise of protecting the *course* when, in fact, the practical effect is just the opposite – they permit moving the ball to the best turf, from which divots are then taken to injure the *course* further.
3. "Preferred lies" or "winter rules" tend generally to lower scores and handicaps, thus penalising the players in competition

with players whose scores for handicaps are made under the Rules of Golf.

4. Extended use or indiscriminate use of "preferred lies" or "winter rules" will place players at a disadvantage when competing at a *course* where the ball must be played as it lies.

c Aeration Holes

When a *course* has been aerated, a Local Rule permitting relief, without penalty, from an aeration hole may be warranted. The following Local Rule is recommended:

"*Through the green*, a ball which comes to rest in or on an aeration hole may be lifted without penalty, cleaned and dropped, as near as possible to the spot where it lay but not nearer the *hole*. The ball when dropped must first strike a part of the *course through the green*.

On the *putting green*, the player shall place the ball at the nearest spot not nearer the *hole* which avoids such situation.

PENALTY FOR BREACH OF LOCAL RULE: *Match play – Loss of hole; Stroke play – Two strokes.*"

4 STONES IN BUNKERS

Stones are, by Definition, *loose impediments* and, when a player's ball is in a *hazard*, a stone lying in or touching the *hazard* may not be touched or moved (Rule 13-4). However, stones in *bunkers* may represent a danger to players (a player could be injured by a stone struck by the player's club in an attempt to play the ball) and they may interfere with the proper playing of the game.

When permission to lift a stone in a *bunker* would be warranted, the following Local Rule is recommended:

"Stones in *bunkers* are movable *obstructions* (Rule 24-1 applies)."

5 FIXED SPRINKLER HEADS

Rule 24-2 provides relief without penalty from interference by an immovable *obstruction*, but it also provides that, except on the *putting green*, intervention on the *line of play* is not, of itself, interference under this Rule.

However, on some courses, the aprons of the *putting greens* are so closely mown that players may wish to putt from just off the green. In such conditions, fixed sprinkler heads on the apron may interfere with the proper playing of the game and the introduction of the following Local Rule providing additional relief without penalty from intervention by a fixed sprinkler head would be warranted:

"All fixed sprinkler heads are immovable *obstructions* and relief from interference by them may be obtained under Rule 24-2. In addition, if a ball lies off the *putting green* but not in a *hazard* and such an *obstruction* on or within two club-lengths of the *putting green* and within two club-lengths of the ball intervenes on the *line of play* between the ball and the *hole*, the player may take relief as follows: The ball shall be lifted and dropped at the nearest point to where the ball lay which (a) is not nearer the *hole*, (b) avoids such intervention and (c) is not in a *hazard* or on a *putting green*. The ball may be cleaned when so lifted.

PENALTY FOR BREACH OF LOCAL RULE: *Match play — Loss of hole; Stroke play — Two strokes.*"

6 TEMPORARY OBSTRUCTIONS

When temporary *obstructions* are installed on or adjoining the *course*, the *Committee* should define the status of such *obstructions* as movable, immovable or temporary immovable *obstructions*.

a Temporary Immovable Obstructions

If the *Committee* defines such *obstructions* as temporary immovable *obstructions*, the following Local Rule is recommended:

"I. Definition

A temporary immovable *obstruction* is a non-permanent artificial object which is often erected in conjunction with a competition and which is fixed or not readily movable.

Examples of temporary immovable *obstructions* include, but are not limited to, tents, scoreboards, grandstands, television towers and lavatories.

Supporting guy wires are part of the temporary immovable *obstruction* unless the *Committee* declares that they are to be treated as elevated power lines or cables.

II. Interference

Interference by a temporary immovable *obstruction* occurs when (a) the ball lies in front of and so close to the *obstruction* that the *obstruction* interferes with the player's *stance* or the area of his intended swing, or (b) the ball lies in, on, under or behind the *obstruction* so that any part of the *obstruction* intervenes directly between the player's ball and the *hole*; interference also exists if the ball lies within one club-length of a spot where such intervention would exist.

Note: A ball is under a temporary immovable *obstruction* when it is below the outer most edges of the *obstruction*, even if these edges do not extend downwards to the ground.

III. Relief

A player may obtain relief from interference by a temporary immovable *obstruction*, including a temporary immovable *obstruction* which is *out of bounds*, as follows:

(a) **Through the Green:** If the ball lies *through the green*, the point on the *course* nearest to where the ball lies shall be determined which (a) is not nearer the *hole*, (b) avoids interference as defined in Clause 2 and (c) is not in a *hazard* or on a *putting green*. The player shall lift the ball and drop it without penalty within one club-length of the point thus determined on a part of the *course* which fulfils (a), (b) and (c) above.

(b) **In a Hazard:** If the ball is in a *hazard*, the player shall lift and drop the ball either:

(i) Without penalty, in the *hazard*, on the nearest part of the *course* affording complete relief within the limits specified in Clause 3a above or, if complete relief is impossible, on a part of the *course* within the *hazard* which affords maximum available relief; or

(ii) **Under the penalty of one stroke**, outside the *hazard* as follows: the point on the *course* nearest to where the ball lies shall be determined which (a) is not nearer the *hole*, (b) avoids interference as defined in Clause 2 and (c) is not in a *hazard*. The player shall drop the ball within one club-length of the point thus determined on a

If there are temporary immovable obstructions, such as TV towers, on the course, the Committee should introduce a Local Rule providing for relief from such temporary immovable obstructions.

part of the *course* which fulfils (a), (b) and (c) above.

The ball may be cleaned when lifted under Clause 3.

Note 1: If the ball lies in a *hazard*, nothing in this Local Rule precludes the player from proceeding under Rule 26 or Rule 28, if applicable.

Note 2: If the ball to be dropped under this Local Rule is not immediately recoverable, another ball may be substituted.

Note 3: A *Committee* may make a Local Rule (a) permitting or requiring a player to use a dropping zone or ball drop when taking relief from a temporary immovable *obstruction* or (b) permitting a player, as an additional relief option, to drop the ball on the opposite side of the *obstruction* from the point established under Clause 3, but otherwise in accordance with Clause 3.

Exceptions:

If a player's ball lies in front of or behind the temporary immovable *obstruction* (not in, on or under the *obstruction*) he may not obtain relief under Clause 3 if:

1. It is clearly unreasonable for him to play a *stroke* or, in the case of intervention, to play a *stroke* such that the ball could finish on a direct line to the *hole*, because of interference by anything other than the temporary immovable *obstruction*;

2. Interference by the temporary immovable

obstruction would occur only through use of an unnecessarily abnormal *stance*, swing or direction of play; or

3. In the case of intervention, it would be clearly unreasonable to expect the player to be able to strike the ball far enough towards the *hole* to reach the temporary immovable *obstruction*.

Note: A player not entitled to relief due to these exceptions may proceed under Rule 24-2.

IV. Ball Lost

If there is reasonable evidence that the ball is *lost* in, on or under a temporary immovable *obstruction*, a ball may be dropped under the provisions of Clause 3 or Clause 5, if applicable. For the purpose of applying Clauses 3 and 5, the ball shall be deemed to lie at the spot where it last entered the *obstruction* (Rule 24-2c).

V. Dropping Zones (Ball Drops)

If the player has interference from a temporary immovable *obstruction*, the *Committee* may permit or require the use of a dropping zone or ball drop. If the player uses a dropping zone in taking relief, he must drop the ball in the dropping zone nearest to where his ball originally lay or is deemed to lie under Clause 4 (even though the nearest dropping zone may be nearer the *hole*).

Note 1: A *Committee* may make a Local Rule prohibiting the use of a dropping zone or ball drop which is nearer the *hole*.

Note 2: If the ball is dropped in a dropping zone, the ball shall not be re-dropped if it comes to rest within two club-lengths of the spot where it first struck a part of the *course* even though it may come to rest nearer the *hole* or outside the boundaries of the dropping zone.

PENALTY FOR BREACH OF LOCAL RULE: *Match play – Loss of hole; Stroke play – Two strokes.*"

b Temporary Power Lines and Cables

When temporary power lines, cables, or telephone lines are installed on the *course*, the following Local Rule is recommended:
"Temporary power lines, cables, telephone lines and mats covering or stanchions supporting them are *obstructions*:

1. If they are readily movable, Rule 24-1 applies.
2. If they are fixed or not readily movable, the player may, if the ball lies *through the green* or in a *bunker*, obtain relief as provided in Rule 24-2b. If the ball lies in a *water hazard*, the player may lift and drop the ball in accordance with Rule 24-2b(i) except that the *nearest point of relief* must be in the *water hazard* and the ball must be dropped in the *water hazard* or the player may proceed under Rule 26.
3. If a ball strikes an elevated power line or cable, the *stroke* shall be cancelled and replayed, without penalty (see Rule 20-5). If the ball is not immediately recoverable another ball may be substituted.
   Note: Guy wires supporting a temporary immovable *obstruction* are part of the temporary immovable *obstruction* unless the *Committee*, by Local Rule, declares that they are to be treated as elevated power lines or cables.
   Exception: Ball striking elevated junction section of cable rising from the ground shall not be replayed.
4. Grass-covered cable trenches are *ground under repair* even if not so marked and Rule 25-1b applies."

PART C: CONDITIONS OF THE COMPETITION

Rule 33-1 provides, "The *Committee* shall lay down the conditions under which a competition is to be played." Such conditions should include many matters such as method of entry, eligibility, number of rounds to be played, etc. which it is not appropriate to deal with in the Rules of Golf or this Appendix. Detailed information regarding such conditions is provided in "Decisions on the Rules of Golf" under Rule 33-1.

However, there are seven matters which might be covered in the Conditions of the Competition to which the *Committee's* attention is specifically drawn by way of a Note to the appropriate Rule. These are:

1. SPECIFICATION OF THE BALL (NOTE TO RULE 5-1)

The following two conditions are recommended only for competitions involving expert players:

a List of Conforming Golf Balls

The USGA periodically issues a List of Conforming Golf Balls which list balls that have been tested and found to conform. If the *Committee* wishes to require use of a brand of golf ball on the List, the List should be posted and the following condition of competition used:

"The ball the player uses shall be named on the current List of Conforming Golf Balls issued by the United States Golf Association.

PENALTY FOR BREACH OF CONDITION: *Disqualification.*"

b One Ball Condition

If it is desired to prohibit changing brands and types of golf balls during a *stipulated round*, the following condition is recommended:

"Limitation on Balls Used During Round: (Note to Rule 5-1)

(i) "One Ball" Condition

During a *stipulated round*, the balls a player uses must be of the same brand and type as detailed by a single entry on the current List of Conforming Golf Balls.

PENALTY FOR BREACH OF CONDITION: *Match play* — At the conclusion of the hole at which the breach is discovered, the state of the match shall be adjusted by deducting one hole for each hole at which a breach occurred; maximum deduction per round: Two holes. *Stroke play* — Two strokes for each hole at which any breach occurred; maximum penalty per round: Four strokes.

(ii) Procedure When Breach Discovered

When a player discovers that he has used a ball in breach of this condition, he shall abandon that ball before playing from the next *teeing ground* and complete the round using a proper ball; otherwise, **the player shall be disqualified**. If discovery is made during play of a hole and the player elects to substitute a proper ball before completing that hole, the player shall place a proper ball on the spot where the ball used in breach of the condition lay."

2 TIME OF STARTING (NOTE TO RULE 6-3a)

If the *Committee* wishes to act in accordance with the Note, the following wording is recommended:

"If the player arrives at his starting point, ready to play, within five minutes after his starting time in the absence of circumstances which warrant waiving the penalty of disqualification as provided in Rule 33-7, the penalty for failure to start on time is loss of the first hole to be played in match play or two strokes in stroke play. Penalty for lateness beyond five minutes is disqualification."

3 PACE OF PLAY

The *Committee* may lay down pace of play guidelines to help prevent slow play, in accordance with Note 2 to Rule 6-7.

4 SUSPENSION OF PLAY DUE TO A DANGEROUS SITUATION (NOTE TO RULE 6-8b)

As there have been many deaths and injuries from lightning on golf courses, all clubs and sponsors of golf competitions are urged to take precautions for the protection of persons against lightning. Attention is called to Rules 6-8 and 33-2d. If the *Committee* desires to adopt the condition in the Note under Rule 6-8b, the following wording is recommended:

"When play is suspended by the *Committee* for a dangerous situation, if the players in a match or group are between the play of two holes, they shall not resume play until the *Committee* has ordered a resumption of play. If they are in the process of playing a hole, they shall discontinue play immediately and shall not thereafter resume play until the *Committee* has ordered a resumption of play. If a player fails to discontinue play immediately, **he shall be disqualified** unless circumstances warrant waiving such penalty as provided in Rule 33-7.

The signal for suspending play due to a

dangerous situation will be a prolonged note of the siren."

The following signals are generally used and it is recommended that all *Committees* do similarly:

Discontinue Play Immediately: One prolonged note of siren.

Discontinue Play: Three consecutive notes of siren, repeated.

Resume Play: Two short notes of siren, repeated.

5 PRACTICE

a General
The *Committee* may make regulations governing practice in accordance with the Note to Rule 7-1, Exception (c) to Rule 7-2, Note 2 to Rule 7 and Rule 33-2c.

b Practice Between Holes (Note 2 to Rule 7)
It is recommended that a condition of competition prohibiting practice putting or chipping on or near the *putting green* of the hole last played is introduced only in stroke play competitions. The following wording is recommended:

"A player shall not play any practice *stroke* on or near the *putting green* of the hole last played. If a practice *stroke* is played on or near the *putting green* of the hole last played, **the player shall incur a penalty of two strokes** at the next hole, except that in the case of the last hole of the round, he incurs the penalty at that hole."

6 ADVICE IN TEAM COMPETITIONS
If the *Committee* wishes to act in accordance with the Note under Rule 8, the following wording is recommended:
"In accordance with the Note to Rule 8 of the Rules of Golf, each team may appoint one person (in addition to the persons from whom *advice* may be asked under the Rule) who may give *advice* to members of that team. Such person **(if it is desired to insert any restriction on who may be nominated insert such restriction here)** shall be identified to the *Committee* before giving *advice*."

7 NEW HOLES
The *Committee* may provide, in accordance with the Note to Rule 33-2b, that the *holes*

143

and *teeing grounds* for a single round competition, being held on more than one day, may be differently situated on each day.

Other conditions of the competition might include:

TRANSPORTATION

If it is desired to require players to walk in a competition, the following condition is recommended:

"Players shall walk at all times during a *stipulated round*.

PENALTY FOR BREACH OF CONDITION:

Match play – At the conclusion of the hole at which the breach is discovered, the state of the match shall be adjusted by deducting one hole for each hole at which a breach occurred. Maximum deduction per round: Two holes.
Stroke play – Two strokes for each hole at which any breach occurred; maximum penalty per round: Four strokes. In the event of a breach between the play of two holes, the penalty applies to the next hole.
Match or stroke play – Use of any unauthorized form of transportation shall be discontinued immediately upon discovery that a breach has occurred. Otherwise, the player shall be disqualified."

HOW TO DECIDE TIES

Rule 33-6 empowers the *Committee* to determine how and when a halved match or a stroke play tie shall be decided. The decision should be published in advance.

The USGA recommends:

Match Play

A match which ends all square should be played off hole by hole until one *side* wins a hole. The play-off should start on the hole where the match began. In a handicap match, handicap stokes should be allowed as in the prescribed round.

Stroke Play

(a) In the event of a tie in a scratch stroke play competition, a play-off is recommended. Such a play-off may be over 18 holes or a smaller number of holes as specified by the *Committee*. If that is not feasible or there is still a tie, a hole-by-hole play-off is recommended.

(b) In the event of a tie in a handicap stroke play competition, a play-off with handicaps is recommended. Such a play-off may be over 18 holes or a smaller number of holes as specified by the *Committee*. If the play-off is less than 18 holes, the percentage of 18 holes to be played should be applied to the players' handicaps to determine their play-off handicaps. Handicap stroke fractions of one-half stroke or more should count as a full stroke and any lesser fraction should be disregarded.

(c) In either a scratch or handicap stroke play competition, if a play-off of any type is not feasible, matching score cards is recommended. The method of matching cards should be announced in advance. An acceptable method of matching cards is to determine the winner on the basis of the best score for the last nine holes. If the tying players have the same score for the last nine, determine the winner on the basis of the last six holes, last three holes and finally the 18th hole. If such a method is used in a handicap stroke play competition, one-half, one-third, one-sixth, etc. of the handicaps should be deducted. Fractions should not be disregarded. If such a method is used in a competition with a multiple tee start, it is recommended that the "last nine holes, last six holes, etc." is considered to be holes 10-18, 13-18, etc.

(d) If the conditions of the competition provide that ties shall be decided over the last nine, last six, last three and last hole, they should also provide what will happen if this procedure does not produce a winner.

DRAW FOR MATCH PLAY

Although the draw for match play may be completely blind or certain players may be distributed through different quarters or eighths, the General Numerical Draw is recommended if matches are determined by a qualifying round.

General Numerical Draw

For purposes of determining places in the draw, ties in qualifying rounds other than those for the last qualifying place shall be decided by the order in which scores are returned, with the first score to be returned receiving the lowest available number, etc.

If it is impossible to determine the order in which scores are returned, ties shall be determined by a blind draw.

UPPER HALF	LOWER HALF	UPPER HALF	LOWER HALF
64 QUALIFIERS		32 QUALIFIERS	
1 vs 64	2 vs 63	1 vs 32	2 vs 31
32 vs 33	31 vs 34	16 vs 17	15 vs 18
16 vs 49	15 vs 50	8 vs 25	7 vs 26
17 vs 48	18 vs 47	9 vs 24	10 vs 23
8 vs 57	7 vs 58	4 vs 29	3 vs 30
25 vs 40	26 vs 39	13 vs 20	14 vs 19
9 vs 56	10 vs 55	5 vs 28	6 vs 27
24 vs 41	23 vs 42	12 vs 21	11 vs 22
4 vs 61	3 vs 62	16 QUALIFIERS	
29 vs 36	30 vs 35	1 vs 16	2 vs 15
13 vs 52	14 vs 51	8 vs 9	7 vs 10
20 vs 45	19 vs 46	4 vs 13	3 vs 14
5 vs 60	6 vs 59	5 vs 12	6 vs 11
28 vs 37	27 vs 38	8 QUALIFIERS	
12 vs 53	11 vs 54	1 vs 8	2 vs 7
21 vs 44	22 vs 43	4 vs 5	3 vs 6

APPENDICES II & III

Any design in a club or ball which is not covered by Rules 4 and 5 and Appendices II and III, or which might significantly change the nature of the game, will be ruled on by the United States Golf Association.

The dimensions contained in Appendices II and III are referenced in imperial measurements. A metric conversion is also referenced for information, calculated using a conversion rate of 1 inch = 25.4 mm. In the event of any dispute over the conformity of a club or ball, the imperial measurements shall take precedence.

APPENDIX II

DESIGN OF CLUBS

A player in doubt as to the conformity of a club should consult the United States Golf Association.

A manufacturer should submit to the United States Golf Association a sample of a club which is to be manufactured for a ruling as to whether the club conforms with the *Rules*. If a manufacturer fails to submit a sample before manufacturing and/or marketing the club, the manufacturer assumes the risk of a ruling that the club does not conform with the *Rules*. Any sample submitted to the United States Golf Association will become its property for reference purposes.

The following paragraphs prescribe general regulations for the design of clubs, together with specifications and interpretations.

Where a club, or part of a club, is required to have some specific property, this means that it must be designed and manufactured with the intention of having that property. The finished club or part must have that property within manufacturing tolerances appropriate to the material used.

1 CLUBS
a General
A club is an implement designed to be used for striking the ball and generally comes in three forms: woods, irons and putters distinguished by shape and intended use. A putter is a club with a loft not exceeding ten degrees designed primarily for use on the *putting green*.

The club shall not be substantially different from the traditional and customary form and make. The club shall be composed of a shaft and a head. All parts of the club shall be fixed so that the club is one unit, and it shall have no external attachments except as otherwise permitted by the *Rules*.

b Adjustability
Woods and irons shall not be designed to be adjustable except for weight. Putters may be designed to be adjustable for weight and some other forms of adjustability are also permitted. All methods of adjustment permitted by the *Rules* require that:
(i)   the adjustment cannot be readily made;
(ii) all adjustable parts are firmly fixed and there is no reasonable likelihood of them working loose during a round; and
(iii) all configurations of adjustment conform with the *Rules*.

The disqualification penalty for purposely changing the playing characteristics of a club during a *stipulated round* (Rule 4-2a) applies to all clubs including a putter.

c Length
The overall length of the club shall be at least 18 inches (457.2mm) measured from the top of the grip along the axis of the shaft or a straight line extension of it to the sole of the club.

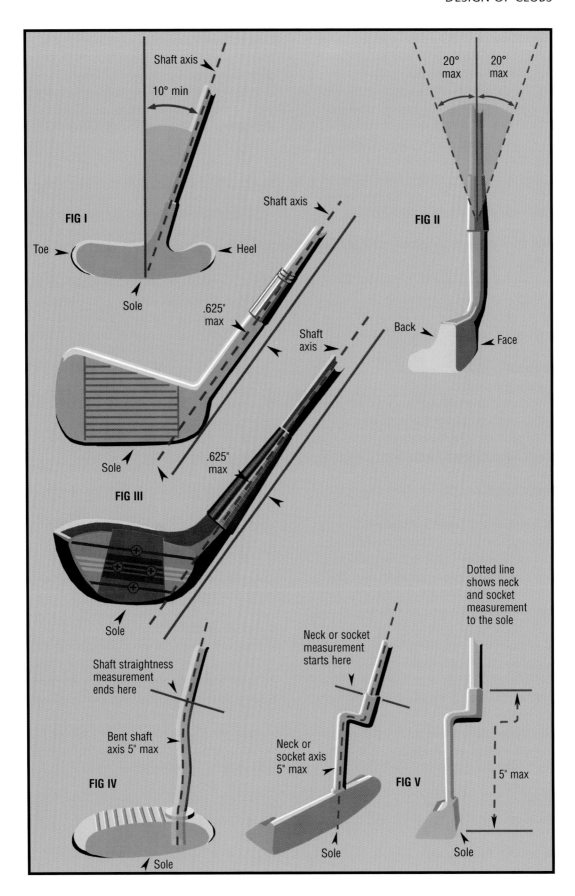

FIG I

Shaft axis
10° min
Toe
Heel
Sole

FIG II

20° max
20° max
Back
Face

FIG III

Shaft axis
.625" max
Shaft axis
.625" max
Sole
Sole

FIG IV

Shaft straightness measurement ends here
Bent shaft axis 5" max
Sole

FIG V

Neck or socket measurement starts here
Neck or socket axis 5" max
Sole

Dotted line shows neck and socket measurement to the sole
5" max
Sole

d Alignment

When the club is in its normal address position the shaft shall be so aligned that:

(i) the projection of the straight part of the shaft on to the vertical plane through the toe and heel shall diverge from the vertical by at least 10 degrees (see Fig. I);

(ii) the projection of the straight part of the shaft on to the vertical plane along the intended line of play shall not diverge from the vertical by more than 20 degrees (see Fig. II).

Except for putters, all of the heel portion of the club shall lie within 0.625 inches (15.88 mm) of the plane containing the axis of the straight part of the shaft and the intended (horizontal) line of play (see Fig. III).

2 SHAFT

a Straightness

The shaft shall be straight from the top of the grip to a point not more than 5 inches (127 mm) above the sole, measured from the point where the shaft ceases to be straight along the axis of the bent part of the shaft and the neck and/or socket (see Fig. IV).

b Bending and Twisting Properties

At any point along its length, the shaft shall:

(i) bend in such a way that the deflection is the same regardless of how the shaft is rotated about its longitudinal axis; and

(ii) twist the same amount in both directions.

c Attachment to Clubhead

The shaft shall be attached to the clubhead at the heel either directly or through a single plain neck and/or socket. The length from the top of the neck and/or socket to the sole of the club shall not exceed 5 inches (127mm), measured along the axis of, and following any bend in, the neck and/or socket (see Fig. V).

Exception for Putters: The shaft or neck or socket of a putter may be fixed at any point in the head.

3 GRIP (SEE FIG. VI)

The grip consists of material added to the shaft to enable the player to obtain a firm hold. The grip shall be straight and plain in form, shall extend to the end of the shaft and shall not be molded for any part of the hands. If no material is added, that portion of the shaft designed to be held by the player shall be considered the grip.

(i) For clubs other than putters the grip must be circular in cross-section, except that a continuous, straight, slightly raised rib may be incorporated along the full length of the grip, and a slightly indented spiral is permitted on a wrapped grip or a replica of one.

(ii) A putter grip may have a non-circular cross-section, provided the cross-section has no concavity, is symmetrical and remains generally similar throughout the length of the grip. (See Clause (v) below).

(iii) The grip may be tapered but must not have any bulge or waist. Its cross-sectional dimensions measured in any direction must not exceed 1.75 inches (44.45mm).

(iv) For clubs other than putters the axis of the grip must coincide with the axis of the shaft.

(v) A putter may have two grips provided each is circular in cross-section, the axis of each coincides with the axis of the shaft, and they are separated by at least 1.5 inches (38.1mm).

4 CLUBHEAD

a Plain in Shape

The clubhead shall be generally plain in shape. All parts shall be rigid, structural in nature and functional. It is not practicable to define plain in shape precisely and comprehensively but features which are deemed to be in breach of this requirement and are therefore not permitted include:

(i) holes through the head,

(ii) transparent material added for other than decorative or structural purposes,

(iii) appendages to the main body of the head such as knobs, plates, rods or fins, for the purpose of meeting dimensional

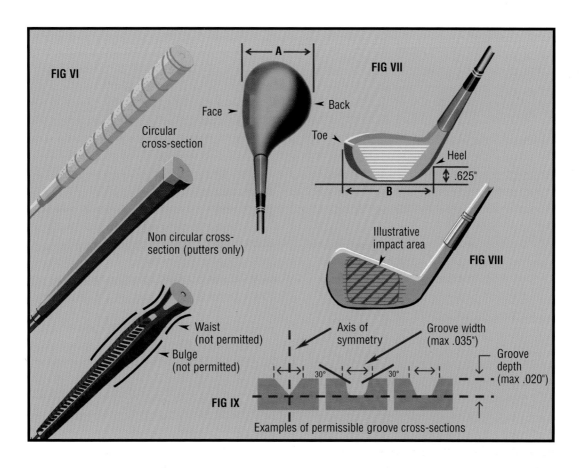

FIG VI

Face ➤

Circular cross-section

Non circular cross-section (putters only)

◄ A ►

◄ Back

FIG VII

Toe

Heel

.625"

◄ B ►

Illustrative impact area

FIG VIII

Waist (not permitted)

Bulge (not permitted)

Axis of symmetry

Groove width (max .035")

Groove depth (max .020")

30° 30°

FIG IX

Examples of permissible groove cross-sections

---

specifications, for aiming or for any other purpose. Exceptions may be made for putters.

Any furrows in or runners on the sole shall not extend into the face.

b Dimensions

The distance from the heel to the toe of the clubhead shall be greater than the distance from the face to the back. These dimensions are measured, with the clubhead in its normal address position, on horizontal lines between vertical projections of the outermost points of (i) the heel and the toe and (ii) the face and the back (see Fig. VII, dimension A). If the outermost point of the heel is not clearly defined, it is deemed to be 0.625 inches (15.88mm) above the horizontal plane on which the club is resting in its normal address position (see Fig. VII, dimension B).

c Striking Faces

The clubhead shall only have one striking face, except that a putter may have two such faces if their characteristics are the same, and they are opposite each other.

5 CLUB FACE

a General

The material and construction of, or any treatment to, the face or clubhead shall not have the effect at impact of a spring (test on file), or impart significantly more spin to the ball than a standard steel face, or have any other effect which would unduly influence the movement of the ball.

The face of the club shall be hard and rigid (some exceptions may be made for putters) and, except for such markings listed below, shall be smooth and shall not have any degree of concavity.

b Impact Area Roughness and Material

Except for markings specified in the following paragraphs, the surface roughness within the area where impact is intended (the "impact

149

area") must not exceed that of decorative sandblasting, or of fine milling (see Fig. VIII).

The whole of the impact area must be of the same material. Exceptions may be made for wooden clubs.

c Impact Area Markings

Markings in the impact area must not have sharp edges or raised lips as determined by a finger test. Grooves or punch marks in the impact area must meet the following specifications:

(i) **Grooves.** A series of straight grooves with diverging sides and a symmetrical cross-section may be used (see Fig. IX). The width and cross-section must be consistent across the face of the club and along the length of the grooves. Any rounding of groove edges shall be in the form of a radius which does not exceed 0.020 inches (0.508 mm). The width of the grooves shall not exceed 0.035 inches (0.9mm), using the 30 degree method of measurement on file with the United States Golf Association. The distance between edges of adjacent grooves must not be less than three times the width of a groove, and not less than 0.075 inches (1.905mm). The depth of a groove must not exceed 0.020 inches (0.508mm).
   Note: Exception — see US Decision 4-1/100.

(ii) **Punch Marks.** Punch marks may be used. The area of any such mark must not exceed 0.0044 square inches (2.84 sq. mm). A mark must not be closer to an adjacent mark than 0.168 inches (4.27 mm) measured from center to center. The depth of a punch mark must not exceed 0.040 inches (1.02 mm). If punch marks are used in combination with grooves, a punch mark must not be closer to a groove than 0.168 inches (4.27 mm), measured from center to center.

d Decorative Markings

The center of the impact area may be indicated by a design within the boundary of a square whose sides are 0.375 inches (9.53 mm) in length. Such a design must not unduly influence the movement of the ball. Decorative markings are permitted outside the impact area.

e Non-metallic Club Face Markings

The above specifications apply to clubs on which the impact area of the face is of metal or a material of similar hardness. They do not apply to clubs with faces made of other materials and whose loft angle is 24 degrees or less, but markings which could unduly influence the movement of the ball are prohibited. Clubs with this type of face and a loft angle exceeding 24 degrees may have grooves of maximum width 0.040 inches (1.02 mm) and maximum depth 1½ times the groove width, but must otherwise conform to the markings specifications above.

f Putter Face

The specifications above with regard to roughness, material and markings in the impact area do not apply to putters.

APPENDIX III

THE BALL

1 WEIGHT

The weight of the ball shall not be greater than 1.620 ounces avoirdupois (45.93 gm).

2 SIZE

The diameter of the ball shall be not less than 1.680 inches (42.67mm). This specification will be satisfied if, under its own weight, a ball falls through a 1.680 inches diameter ring gauge in fewer than 25 out of 100 randomly selected positions, the test being carried out at a temperature of 23 ± 1°C.

3 SPHERICAL SYMMETRY

The ball must not be designed, manufactured or intentionally modified to have properties which differ from those of a spherically symmetrical ball.

4 INITIAL VELOCITY

The initial velocity of the ball shall not exceed the limit specified (test on file) when measured on apparatus approved by the United States Golf Association.

5 OVERALL DISTANCE STANDARD

The combined carry and roll of the ball, when tested on apparatus approved by the United States Golf Association, shall not exceed the distance specified under the conditions set forth in the Overall Distance Standard for golf balls on file with the United States Golf Association.

PHOTOGRAPHIC ACKNOWLEDGEMENTS

Allsport 98 left, / David Cannon 12, 30, 88, / Graham Chadwick 110 bottom, / Phil Cole 129, /Craig Jones 89, / Stephen Munday 7 bottom, /Andrew Redington 31
Peter Dazeley 24 left, 98 right
Joann Dost Golf Editions / Joann Dost 68 bottom
Phil Sheldon Golf Picture Library: 7 top, 24 right, 50 top, 58, 95 top, 108, 135, 140
United States Golf Association 27 bottom